# PROGRAMMING WITH GENERATORS
An Introduction

**ELLIS HORWOOD SERIES IN COMPUTERS AND THEIR APPLICATIONS**
*Series Editor:* IAN CHIVERS, Senior Analyst, The Computer Centre, King's College, London, and formerly Senior Programmer and Analyst, Imperial College of Science and Technology, University of London

| | |
|---|---|
| Abramsky, S. & Hankin, C.J. | ABSTRACT INTERPRETATION OF DECLARATIVE LANGUAGES |
| Alexander, H. | FORMALLY-BASED TOOLS AND TECHNIQUES FOR HUMAN–COMPUTER DIALOGUES |
| Atherton, R. | STRUCTURED PROGRAMMING WITH BBC BASIC |
| Atherton, R. | STRUCTURED PROGRAMMING WITH COMAL |
| Baeza-Yates, R.A. | TEXT SEARCHING ALGORITHMS |
| Bailey, R. | FUNCTIONAL PROGRAMMING WITH HOPE |
| Barrett, R., Ramsay, A. & Sloman, A. | POP-11 |
| Berztiss, A. | PROGRAMMING WITH GENERATORS |
| Bharath, R. | COMPUTERS AND GRAPH THEORY |
| Bishop, P. | FIFTH GENERATION COMPUTERS |
| Bullinger, H.-J. & Gunzenhauser, H. | SOFTWARE ERGONOMICS |
| Burns, A. | NEW INFORMATION TECHNOLOGY |
| Carberry, J.C. | COBOL |
| Carlini, U. & Villano, U. | TRANSPUTERS AND PARALLEL ARCHITECTURES |
| Chivers, I.D. | AN INTRODUCTION TO STANDARD PASCAL |
| Chivers, I.D. | MODULA 2 |
| Chivers, I.D. & Sleighthome, J. | INTERACTIVE FORTRAN 77 |
| Clark, M.W. | PC-PORTABLE FORTRAN |
| Clark, M.W. | TEX |
| Cockshott, W. P. | PS-ALGOL IMPLEMENTATIONS: Applications in Persistent Object-Oriented Programming |
| Colomb, R. | IMPLEMENTING PERSISTENT PROLOG |
| Cope, T. | COMPUTING USING BASIC |
| Curth, M.A. & Edelmann, H. | APL |
| Dahlstrand, I. | SOFTWARE PORTABILITY AND STANDARDS |
| Dongarra, J., Duff, I., Gaffney, P., & McKee, S. | VECTOR AND PARALLEL COMPUTING |
| Dunne, P.E. | COMPUTABILITY THEORY |
| Eastlake, J.J. | A STRUCTURED APPROACH TO COMPUTER STRATEGY |
| Eisenbach, S. | FUNCTIONAL PROGRAMMING |
| Ellis, D. | MEDICAL COMPUTING AND APPLICATIONS |
| Ennals, J.R. | ARTIFICIAL INTELLIGENCE |
| Ennals, J.R. | BEGINNING MICRO-PROLOG |
| Ennals, J.R., *et al.* | INFORMATION TECHNOLOGY AND EDUCATION |
| Filipič, B. | PROLOG USER'S HANDBOOK |
| Ford, N. | COMPUTER PROGRAMMING LANGUAGES |
| Guariso, G. & Werthner, H. | ENVIRONMENTAL DECISION SUPPORT SYSTEMS |
| Harland, D.M. | CONCURRENCY AND PROGRAMMING LANGUAGES |
| Harland, D.M. | POLYMORPHIC PROGRAMMING LANGUAGES |
| Harland, D.M. | REKURSIV |
| Harris, D.J. | DEVELOPING DEDICATED DBASE SYSTEMS |
| Henshall, J. & Shaw, S. | OSI EXPLAINED, 2nd Edition |
| Hepburn, P.H. | FURTHER PROGRAMMING IN PROLOG |
| Hepburn, P.H. | PROGRAMMING IN MICRO-PROLOG MADE SIMPLE |
| Hill, I.D. & Meek, B.L. | PROGRAMMING LANGUAGE STANDARDISATION |
| Hirschheim, R., Smithson, S. & Whitehouse, D. | MICROCOMPUTERS AND THE HUMANITIES: Survey and Recommendations |
| Hutchins, W.J. | MACHINE TRANSLATION |
| Hutchison, D. | FUNDAMENTALS OF COMPUTER LOGIC |
| Hutchison, D. & Silvester, P. | COMPUTER LOGIC |
| Koopman, P. | STACK COMPUTERS |
| Kenning, M.-M. & Kenning, M.J. | COMPUTERS AND LANGUAGE LEARNING: Current Theory and Practice |
| Koskimies, K. & Paaki, J. | AUTOMATING LANGUAGE IMPLEMENTATION |
| Koster, C.H.A. | TOP-DOWN PROGRAMMING WITH ELAN |
| Last, R. | ARTIFICIAL INTELLIGENCE TECHNIQUES IN LANGUAGE LEARNING |
| Lester, C. | A PRACTICAL APPROACH TO DATA STRUCTURES |
| Lucas, R. | DATABASE APPLICATIONS USING PROLOG |
| Lucas, A. | DESKTOP PUBLISHING |
| Maddix, F. & Morgan, G. | SYSTEMS SOFTWARE |
| Matthews, J.L. | FORTH |
| Millington, D. | SYSTEMS ANALYSIS AND DESIGN FOR COMPUTER APPLICATIONS |
| Moseley, L.G., Sharp, J.A. & Salenieks, P. | PASCAL IN PRACTICE |
| Moylan, P. | ASSEMBLY LANGUAGE FOR ENGINEERS |
| Narayanan, A. & Sharkey, N.E. | AN INTRODUCTION TO LISP |
| Parrington, N. & Roper, M. | UNDERSTANDING SOFTWARE TESTING |
| Paterson, A. | OFFICE SYSTEMS |
| Phillips, C. & Cornelius, B.J. | COMPUTATIONAL NUMERICAL METHODS |
| Rahtz, S.P.Q. | INFORMATION TECHNOLOGY IN THE HUMANITIES |
| Ramsden, E. | MICROCOMPUTERS IN EDUCATION 2 |

*Series continued at back of book*

# PROGRAMMING WITH GENERATORS
## An Introduction

**ALFS BERZTISS** M.Sc., Ph.D.
**Department of Computer Science**
**University of Pittsburgh, USA**
**and SYSLAB, University of Stockholm**

**ELLIS HORWOOD**
NEW YORK  LONDON  TORONTO  SYDNEY  TOKYO  SINGAPORE

First published in 1990 by
**ELLIS HORWOOD LIMITED**
Market Cross House, Cooper Street,
Chichester, West Sussex, PO19 1EB, England

A division of
Simon & Schuster International Group

© Ellis Horwood Limited, 1990

All rights reserved. No part of this publication may be
reproduced, stored in a retrieval system, or transmitted,
in any form, or by any means, electronic, mechanical,
photocopying, recording or otherwise, without the prior
permission, in writing, of the publisher

Printed and bound in Great Britain
by Bookcraft (Bath) Limited, Midsomer Norton

**British Library Cataloguing in Publication Data**
Berztiss, Alfs
Programming with generators: an introduction.
1. Computer systems. Software
I. Title
005.3
ISBN 0–13–739087–4

**Library of Congress Cataloging-in-Publication Data available**

# Contents

Preface  7

1. Functions and Generators  9
   1.1  A classification of software  9
   1.2  From constants to generators  13
   1.3  A heapsort generator  17
   1.4  Generators for binary tree traversal  24
   1.5  The verification and validation obligation  31
   1.6  Development of a generator for preorder traversal  36
   1.7  The Towers of Hanoi  41
   1.8  A study of inorder traversal  45
   1.9  Summary of properties of generators  50

2. Applications of Generators  53
   2.1  Intermeshed binary tree traversals  53
   2.2  A text formatter  57
   2.3  Sorting and the two-way merge  66
   2.4  Updating of files  78
   2.5  A spelling checker  86
   2.6  The problem of doubled characters  89
   2.7  Multiplication of matrices  92

3. The Generate-and-Test Paradigm  101
   3.1  The queens problem  101
   3.2  Backtracking  109
   3.3  A shortest path problem  112
   3.4  The queens problem revisited  115
   3.5  More problems based on permutations  118
   3.6  And once more the queens problem  122
   3.7  The $A^*$-algorithm  126
   3.8  A case study: diagnostic inference  128

4. Implementation of Generators   139
   4.1 Simulation of generators   139
   4.2 An overview of Icon   142
   4.3 Generators in Icon   150
   4.4 Backtracking and Icon generators   156
   4.5 The Lucid language   160
   4.6 Unix pipes and lazy evaluation   165
   4.7 Data flow computation   166

Appendix A: Exercises   171

Appendix B: Bibliographic notes   177

Appendix C: Bibliography   181

Index   189

# Preface

Our outlook on software development is undergoing a radical change. The use of formal specification languages, such as VDM and Z, and non-traditional programming languages, such as Lisp and Prolog, is spreading from academic research establishments into industrial environments. Also, there has come the realization that the diverse problems for which we seek software solutions cannot all be approached in the same way. The emerging paradigm is one of prototype-based software development in which languages and techniques are selected and combined on the basis of how well they match the problems to be solved and how well they support validation and verification. Specialization of programming languages and techniques should be welcomed as evidence of the maturing of the sciences of computation. But, as software development evolves into a collection of approaches, we must determine when and where to use a particular approach, develop appropriate techniques for the different approaches, and establish methodologies of validation and verification for each approach. This book begins to do so for programming with generators.

My interest in generators began with a very practical problem relating to critical path analysis: I had to find a way to synchronize two simultaneous traversals of a binary tree representation of a scheduling network. Indeed, most of Chapter 2 of this book addresses practical problems, and I wish I could have related every example to a problem of practical significance. Unfortunately most practical problems are too large for books. Hence I had to resort to old stand-bys such as the Towers of Hanoi and the 8-queens problem. I chose to emphasize the 8-queens problem because it is extensively discussed in programming literature.

Languages that explicitly provide generators are very few, and they are not often taught in programming courses. However, I hope that the text will show that design in terms of generators is the natural approach to the development of some types of software, even though the generators may become converted to conventional procedures during the implementation of the design.

This book, then, is an introduction to generators. It can also serve as an introduction to backtrack programming. Occasionally I felt the temptation to include some biased opinions about software development in general. The reader will find that I have not always resisted the temptation. I hope that the book will provide the student with new insights into the software development process, the practitioner with a wider choice of options, and the researcher with the motivation for including generators in a broader range of programming languages.

# 1

# Functions and Generators

A generator is similar to a function, but a generator permits some local data to be preserved between calls to the generator. In this chapter we establish a place for generators within a classification of application software, and define generators for several applications. Some generators, such as those that implement binary tree traversals, find application throughout computing, and their verification is an important concern. Verification of generators is therefore discussed as well. The chapter concludes with a summary of the properties of a version of generators developed for this book.

## 1.1 A CLASSIFICATION OF SOFTWARE

Application software is written to manage information, control processes, or transform data, and we would like to speak of information systems, control systems, and data transformers. However, most application systems are hybrids -- for example, an account management system of a bank may have to maintain a data base of account transactions (information management), cause interest to be deposited into accounts and monthly statements to be sent out (control activities), and prepare summaries of the day's activities at the end of each working day (data transformation). Still, we can refer to the components of application systems as information-control systems and data transformers.

Application software makes use of basic data types, such as integers and booleans, and devices, such as stacks and binary trees. It is customary to regard devices as data types as well. Indeed, much can be said for implementing all software as data types, where a data type consists of a set of entities and of operations on the entities.

A data transformer can be considered in two ways. First, we take an object orientation. Under this orientation a data transformer is allocated as an operation to some data type. For example, matrix multiplication is regarded as the generation of a new element of the set of matrices (the product matrix) from two existing elements of the set. The other is a stream orientation, and we speak then of a *data stream transformer*. This is a procedure that acts on a stream as a whole rather than on individual items. Data stream transformers accept data streams and generate outputs that are again data streams (e.g., a text formatter, a parser, a sorter, or a spelling checker) or that are much compressed (the count of zero elements of a matrix).

The last example shows that the elements of a matrix can be regarded as constituting a data stream. Indeed, matrix multiplication can be interpreted as a data stream transformation as well. Consider two $n \times n$ matrices $A$ and $B$. Let them be represented by two streams -- $A$ by $n$ concatenated sequences of all its elements in row order, and $B$ by $n$ concatenations of its first column, followed by $n$ concatenations of its second column, and so forth. When $n = 2$, we have

$$a_{11} \quad a_{12} \quad a_{21} \quad a_{22} \quad a_{11} \quad a_{12} \quad a_{21} \quad a_{22}$$
$$b_{11} \quad b_{21} \quad b_{11} \quad b_{21} \quad b_{12} \quad b_{22} \quad b_{12} \quad b_{22}$$

and the output stream is

$$a_{11}b_{11} + a_{12}b_{21} \quad a_{21}b_{11} + a_{22}b_{21} \quad a_{11}b_{12} + a_{12}b_{22} \quad a_{21}b_{12} + a_{22}b_{22}$$

Some data streams represent solutions to problems in their own right, without the additional need to apply a data transformer. An example is the sequence (stream) of moves that solves the Towers of Hanoi problem of Section 1.7. If, in the interests of orderliness, we were to insist that every application is to go into some pigeonhole, these applications could be regarded as instances of data transformation in which the data stream passes through an identity transformer that leaves the stream unchanged.

Advocates of software development based on data types generally think of the operations of a data type as functions, which leads to a second classification of software according to the nature of the functions. The classes are defined by two orthogonal two-way partitions. The first relates to the determination of function values. The function *telephone* can be stored as a table of entries of the form <subscriber, telephone number>, for example <*Berztiss*, 624-8401>, and one finds *telephone(Berztiss)* by looking up the table. On the other hand, the value of *cosine* for a given angle is found by application of a computational rule to the angle. The other partition separates functions into static or non-mutable and dynamic or mutable. A non-mutable function does not change -- for example, the cosine function, or a finite function that supplies the times of sunrise at Pittsburgh for the 365 days of 1997. A mutable function changes. Thus, before I got my present office, *telephone(Berztiss)* had the value 624-6458. Fig. 1.1 shows the classification.

|              | static | dynamic |
|--------------|--------|---------|
| based on look-up | LS | LD |
| based on a rule | RS | RD |

Fig. 1.1 -- A classification of functions

Most functions belong to classes LD and RS. The functions based on look-up usually arise as components of persistent data bases, but arrays are also sometimes interpreted as functions. Thus, a $4 \times 4$ integer array can be regarded as a function from the cartesian product $1..4 \times 1..4$ to the set of integers.

Functions of class RD arise in artificial intelligence, as in programs that play board games. Given the configuration of pieces on the board, a next-move function evaluates the effectiveness of feasible moves and returns as its value the move of greatest effectiveness. However, the program may be designed to learn from past experience, and it would then try and improve the next-move function, or, what is more likely today, a programmer would change the function.

In this book we shall deal with a rather restricted application area, the production and transformation of data streams. Within this area we shall focus on the use of generators, which we regard as closely related to rule-based functions (classes RS and RD), but only static generators will be discussed here. Dynamic generators are based on machine learning, and the coverage of the very complex topic of machine learning is outside the scope of this book.

## 1.2 FROM CONSTANTS TO GENERATORS

Examination of functions shows a progression in complexity. The simplest functions are constants -- when computation is interpreted primarily as function evaluation, constants are regarded as very primitive functions that do not require arguments. In this framework the integer 3 is the value of a constant (zero-argument) function *3*. Another example is the current year function, but this is a mutable constant function that changes its value at midnight in the night of the 31st of December. In more familiar usage, a function $f$ is supplied with an argument $x$, which may be a scalar, a vector, or a more complicated structure, and the value $f(x)$ is obtained.

However, there are computations that do not easily conform to this pattern. They include such common tasks as random number generation and the traversal of binary trees. Here the code segment that carries out the computation may or may not be supplied with an argument, and this code segment is to find the next element in a sequence. Consider the sequence of Fibonacci numbers

$$1 \quad 1 \quad 2 \quad 3 \quad 5 \quad 8 \quad 13 \quad 21 \quad ... \; ,$$

defined by the recurrence scheme

$$f_0 = f_1 = 1, \tag{1.1}$$
$$f_n = f_{n-2} + f_{n-1} \quad (n \geq 2). \tag{1.2}$$

Suppose we were required to write a program that finds, for a given value *bound*, the value of the parameter $k$ such that

$$\sum_{i=0}^{k} f_i < bound \;\land\; \sum_{i=0}^{k+1} f_i \geq bound. \tag{1.3}$$

The most convenient way would be to have a subprogram *fib* that returns the elements of the Fibonacci sequence, in order, one at a time, until their sum reaches *bound*. The summation code is then

$$sum := 0;$$
$$k := 0;$$
**while** $sum < bound$ **do begin**
$$sum := sum + fib;$$
**if** $sum < bound$ **then** $k := k + 1$
**end**

Let us now consider the nature of subprogram *fib*. One possibility is to have global variables *fibminus2* and *fibminus1*, initiated to 0 and 1, respectively. The body of *fib* is then

$$new := fibminus2 + fibminus1;$$
$$fibminus2 := fibminus1;$$
$$fibminus1 := new;$$
$$fib := new$$

This works for all $f_i$ except $f_0$. We need therefore another global variable that works as a switch. It is initiated to true, and is used in the first call of *fib* to give access to a region of code that assigns the value 1 to *fib* and sets the switch to false.

However, good programming practice requires that functions have no side effects, that is, a function should just return a value and not change variables that are not local to it. Otherwise reasoning about the behaviour of the function becomes very complicated.

One alternative is to replace the summation statement in the summation code with

$$sum := sum + fib(k)$$

where *fib* now uses the recurrence scheme (1.1-1.2) to compute $f_k$ from scratch. This approach has to be rejected because it raises the complexity of the computation from

$O(k)$ to $O(k^2)$, where $k$ is the summation limit in (1.3). A variant is to use the solution of the recurrence scheme (1.1-1.2),

$$f_k = \frac{1}{\sqrt{5}}\left[\left[\frac{1+\sqrt{5}}{2}\right]^k - \left[\frac{1-\sqrt{5}}{2}\right]^k\right], \qquad (1.4)$$

to find *fib(k)*. Assuming that the exponentiation function has constant time complexity, the complexity of *fib* has been restored to $O(k)$, but the computational effort at each call of the function is still unnecessarily large.

Subprograms are implemented in such a way that they receive memory allocation for local variables on being activated, but this allocation is lost on leaving the subprogram. For efficient implementation of *fib* we require local persistent memory for *fibminus2* and *fibminus1*. A subprogram that has local persistent memory and at each call supplies the next element of a sequence is called a *generator*.

The critical property of a generator is its persistent memory. Such memory was provided by Algol60 in the form of so-called own variables. Generators can also be implemented in Ada, Modula-2, and other less well established languages. Generators are provided by CLU and Icon, and were to have been part of Alphard, but the latter language remained unimplemented. In CLU generators are tied to for-loops, which restricts their applicability, but Icon generators have no such context restriction. Examples of generators in this book are expressed in a language similar to Pascal.

Our first example of a generator is shown as Prog. 1.1. It is a generator for Fibonacci numbers. Except for a few features that are explained below the syntax should be self-explanatory.

> **generator** *fibonacci*: natural;
>
>     **persistent** *fibminus2*, *fibminus1*: natural;
>
>     **temporary** *t*: natural;
>
> **begin**
>
>     *fibminus2* := 0;
>
>     *fibminus1* := 1;
>
>     **suspend** <1>;
>
>     **while** true **do begin**
>
>         *t* := *fibminus2* + *fibminus1*;
>
>         *fibminus2* := *fibminus1*;
>
>         *fibminus1* := *t*;
>
>         **suspend** <*t*>
>
>     **end**
>
> **end** (* *fibonacci* *)

Prog. 1.1 -- A generator of Fibonacci numbers

Generators are defined similarly to functions and procedures, by providing local declarations and a generator body. The declaration of local variables has two parts. One relates to variables that keep their values between calls of the generator; the other relates to variables that do not have to be persistent. A generator is activated by the first call to it, and it remains active until the block in which it has been declared is deactivated.

On the initial entry, generator *fibonacci* initializes *fibminus2* and *fibminus1*, which will be needed for the next entry. A return is then made via the first suspend statement. The generator returns the value in the angular brackets, namely 1. The type of the return value is defined in the generator heading. When the generator is next called, execution resumes from the statement following the suspend from which the return was made. Here this statement starts a loop. Since the Fibonacci sequence is infinite, the loop is a "do-forever." A generator can contain more than one suspend statement, as in Prog. 1.1, where the second suspend is part of the loop body.

It is feasible that more than one *instance* of a generator is needed at the same time. Instances of generators have therefore to be declared in the block in which they are used. Thus

**gen** *fibx, fiby*: *fibonacci*

identifies *fibx* and *fiby* as instances of the generator *fibonacci*.

## 1.3 A HEAPSORT GENERATOR

Our next example is a data transformation task in which a procedure is combined with a generator, and the procedure and the generator make use of two subsidiary procedures. We consider arrays that have the *heap property*. Given an array $arr[1..n]$ of numbers (or some other data type with the relational operator $\leq$). Array $arr$ has the heap property if

$$\forall\, k:\ 1 < k \leq n\ :\ arr[k] \leq arr[k\ \text{div}\ 2], \tag{1.5}$$

where div is integer division. The array shown below has the heap property:

| 25 | 23 | 20 | 22 | 17 | 18 | 15 | 11 | 19 | 16 |
|----|----|----|----|----|----|----|----|----|----|

It is easy to see whether an array has the heap property by superimposing a binary tree on it. The elements of the array are represented in the tree by nodes that are filled from left to right in order of levels. This correspondence between subscripts of elements of our array and nodes of the tree is shown in the lefthand diagram of Fig. 1.2; the correspondence between element values and nodes is shown in the righthand diagram. In terms of the righthand diagram, the array has a (descending) heap property if the value at any node is less than or equal the value at the parent of this node.

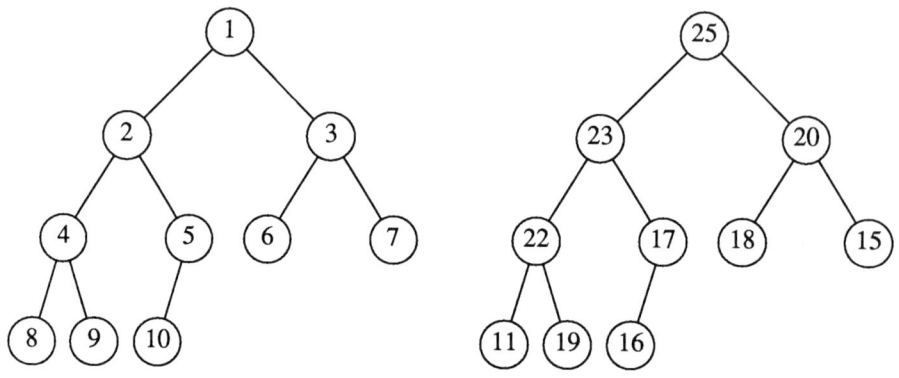

Fig. 1.2 -- The structure of a heap

A data type of heap would be a subtype of an appropriate array type. We need two basic heap maintenance operations. Suppose exactly one value, at node $k$ in the binary tree, is responsible for the heap property not holding. If it is larger that its parent, then it would have to be "bubbled up" until it reaches its appropriate level. If it is smaller than any of its children, then it has to be exchanged with the larger of its children, and so forth down the tree to maintain the heap property. Let these operations be called *bubbleup* and *siftdown*.

We can define a number of processes in terms of the basic operations. For this we propose an array $arr[1..n]$, but sometimes we will consider only the first *topnow* elements of the array as significant. The conversion of an arbitrary array $arr[1..topnow]$ into a heap is accomplished by the code

$limit := topnow$ **div** $2;$

**for** $index := limit$ **downto** $1$ **do**

$siftdown(arr, index, topnow)$

For the addition of a new element to a heap we have

$topnow := topnow + 1;$

$arr[topnow] := newvalue;$

$bubbleup(arr, topnow)$

A very useful sorting process, called *heapsort* is based on the heap property. The process has two stages. The first is the creation of the heap. This can be done in time proportional to the number of elements in the array that is to be converted into a heap. The next stage delivers sorted data at intervals proportional to the logarithm of the number of elements in the heap. The generator of Prog. 1.2 implements this second stage. On the first call it returns $arr[1]$. After this the value at $arr[topnow]$ is moved into $arr[1]$, *topnow* is reduced by one, and the value now at $arr[1]$ is sifted down. This makes the value at $arr[1]$ again the largest of the *topnow* values in the heap. This continues until *topnow* has been reduced to 1. Using a generator here means that the generation of the sorted elements can be overlapped with a process that receives the elements as its input.

> **generator** *heapsort*(*arr*: integerarray; *size*: natural): integer;
>
> **persistent** *topnow*: natural;
>
> **begin**
>
> > **for** *topnow* := *size* **downto** 1 **begin**
> >
> > > **suspend** <*arr*[1]>;
> > >
> > > *arr*[1] := *arr*[*topnow*];
> > >
> > > **if** *topnow* > 2 **then**
> > >
> > > > *siftdown*(*arr*, 1, *topnow*-1)
> >
> > **end**
>
> **end** (* *heapsort* *)

Prog. 1.2 -- A generator for heapsort

The generator of Prog. 1.2 differs from the generator of Fibonacci numbers in some important ways. First, the generator is applied to a structure, and returns the data stored in the structure. Second, *siftdown* changes array *arr*. In Pascal, an argument is passed to a function or a procedure in two modes. When passed in the value mode, any change made to it within the called function or procedure is not visible outside this function or procedure. When passed in the variable mode, the change is visible outside the function or procedure. For example, suppose we have

> **procedure** *square1*(*n*: integer);
>
> **begin**
>
> > *n* := *n* * *n*
>
> **end** (* *square1* *)

and another procedure that differs only in the heading, as follows:

**procedure** *square2*(**var** *n*: integer);

If initially $m = 2$, then $m$ is still 2 after the call *square1*($m$), but it is 4 after the call *square2*($m$).

For a generator we could have three modes of argument passing. The variable mode would correspond exactly to the Pascal variable mode, but we are not going to make use of it. The value mode now becomes two modes. One will be called fixed value mode, the other changing value mode. Under the fixed value mode an argument is passed to a generator only once, at the time the generator is first called. For example, when *arr* is passed into *heapsort*, a local copy is made of it, and all changes to *arr* made by the generator are confined to this copy. If the calling program changes the value of this argument between calls to the generator, the change has no effect on the generator. Whenever possible, arguments should be passed to generators as fixed values. The need for the changing value mode arises when fresh data have to be passed into a generator after the first call. However, a need to pass arguments in the changing value mode will not arise before Section 2.4. Examples of such arguments are provided by Progs. 2.12 and 3.3.

If we were to allow the variable mode, then, when two generators simultaneously access a structure *s*, any structural changes made to *s* by one of the generators could be communicated to the other. This can have benefits at times, but our restriction has greater benefits. For example, a programmer does not have to be concerned that the implementation of a generator may cause temporary changes in the object being traversed, such as the reversal of pointers in stackless traversals of binary trees. Without the restriction verification of programs in which several generators traverse a structure that is being altered by one or more of the generators would be exceedingly difficult.

**generator** *heapsort*(*arr*: array; *size*: natural; *null*: integer): integer;

  **persistent** *topnow*: natural;

**begin**

  **for** *topnow* := *size* **downto** 1 **begin**

    **suspend** <*arr*[1]>;

    *arr*[1] := *arr*[*topnow*];

    **if** *topnow* > 2 **then**

      *siftdown*(*arr*, 1, *topnow*-1)

  **end**;

  **while** true **do suspend** <*null*>

**end** (* *heapsort* *)

Prog. 1.3 -- A "safer" generator for heapsort

The finite nature of a structure traversed by a generator implies that the generator has completed its task after a finite number of calls. For example, with Prog. 1.2, we would know the number of elements in the heap, and could limit the number of calls accordingly, but in general it may be difficult to determine the required number of calls in advance. This raises two problems. One is how to tell when to stop calling a generator. This will be taken up in the next section. The other is what happens when the generator is called after it has returned the last element of the sequence it is to generate. In general we shall adopt the following convention: a generator that has returned all of its sequence should go into a do-forever loop, and, when in this loop, return a null value that is supplied by the caller as an argument. Prog. 1.3 is *heapsort* modified to follow this convention. However (as in Section 2.7), a generator may also start generating its sequence all over again. Under this alternative the generator should go into a do-forever loop when applied to an empty object. An exceptional (error) condition would arise if execution were to reach the end of the definition of a generator.

Although I am a strong believer in computation as function construction, my belief is not total. You will have noticed that the basic operations *siftdown* and *bubbleup* are procedures. The heap creation operation is also best implemented as a procedure. The advantages that functions provide in reasoning about software are for the most part limited to functions that do not change their input arguments. Since the data transformer *bubbleup* has a structure for one of its arguments, and its purpose is precisely to change this structure, it should not be designed as a function.

Suppose that *bubbleup* were a function, and we were to apply it to the 9th element of array *arr*:

| 25 | 23 | 20 | 22 | 17 | 18 | 15 | 11 | 24 | 16 |
|----|----|----|----|----|----|----|----|----|----|

Then *bubbleup* would make a copy of *arr*, bubble up the 24 in this copy, and return the transformed array as its value. However, it is most likely that the returned value would immediately overwrite *arr*:

$$arr := bubbleup\,(arr,\,9) \qquad (1.6)$$

An array would then have been copied unnecessarily twice: within *bubbleup*, and in the execution of assignment statement (1.6). Data transformers are therefore best implemented as procedures. Note that the *intent* here is quite different from that with generator *heapsort* (Progs. 1.2 and 1.3). The whole purpose of *bubbleup* is to change *arr*; the change to *arr* brought about by *heapsort* is incidental to the generation of the output sequence.

## 1.4 GENERATORS FOR BINARY TREE TRAVERSAL

A data structure, that is, a structured data type, comes in two guises. First, it exists in its own right as the embodiment of some relation. Second, a data structure is a carrier of data of some other type. For example, we are rarely interested in a binary tree for its own sake. Rather we are interested in the data stored at its nodes, on which the tree superimposes a particular relation. Suppose we are to access the nodes of a binary tree in preorder and interleave the traversal of the binary tree with some operation on the data stored at the nodes. This requires that the traversal operation be invoked more than once. An important purpose of generators is to take care of such situations.

Prog. 1.4 is an example: generator *preorder* traverses the binary tree identified by *bin* in preorder, and returns the values associated with the nodes of *bin* as they are reached. Argument *null* supplies the value that the generator is to return when it is called after it has completed the traversal. The generator makes use of stack functions *newstack*, *push*, and *pop*, which deliver, respectively, an empty stack, a stack to which an item of type datumtype has been added, and a stack from which the top element has been deleted. In contrast to *bubbleup* and *siftdown* of Section 1.3, these operations have been implemented as functions rather than procedures. This is in keeping with the assumption in specification of abstract data types that all operations of a data type are to be functions. Moreover, functions, when properly applied, avoid side effects. We shall adopt the convention that a function is always to return a single value, which may be a scalar, an array, or a more complicated structure, such as a binary tree, and it is to have no side effects, that is, it is to make no reference to global data, and no change to its arguments is to have an effect outside the function. Function *read* returns the top item in the stack, and predicate *emptystack* determines whether the stack is empty. Availability of the following binary tree functions is also assumed: the predicate *emptytree*, true if the binary tree is empty, functions *left* and *right*, which return the left or right subtree of the argument, respectively, and *datum*, which returns the datum associated with the root of its argument. The evolution of Prog. 1.4 from an initial recursive specification will be traced out in Section 1.6.

    **generator** *preorder*(*bin*: bintreetype; *null*: datumtype): datumtype;

        **persistent** *stack*: stacktype; *node*: bintreetype;

    **begin**

        **if not** *emptytree*(*bin*) **then begin**

            *stack*:= *push*(*newstack*, *bin*);

            **while not** *emptytree*(*node*) **or not** *emptystack*(*stack*) **do begin**

                **if** *emptytree*(*node*) **then begin**

                    *node*:= *read*(*stack*); *stack*:= *pop*(*stack*)

                **end**;

                **suspend** <*datum*(*node*)>;

                **if not** *emptytree*(*right*(*node*)) **then** *stack*:= *push*(*stack*, *right*(*node*));

                *node*:= *left*(*node*)

            **end**

        **end**;

        **while** true **do**

            **suspend** <*null*>

    **end** (* *preorder* *)

        Prog. 1.4 -- Preorder traversal of a binary tree

Generator *preorder* returns the data associated with nodes of a binary tree in the order the nodes are reached under preorder traversal of the binary tree. Sometimes, however, this information is not enough. For example, in a parse tree for a sentence the internal nodes of the tree hold labels of syntactic categories, and the terminal nodes or leaves hold the words of the sentence. Should we be interested only in the latter, we would like the generator to tell us which nodes are terminal.

To make this more general, we shall let the generator return a pair <*v, tag*>, where *v* is the value in which the programmer is primarily interested and *tag* is a tag value. In particular, for a generator that goes through a finite iteration sequence, the ultimate value of *tag* should be F (for Finished), or something similar. For example, when the postorder sequence of a binary tree ends, the generator returns the root of the binary tree and a tag value other than F. If the generator were now to be called again, it should return the tag F coupled to a null value. The other tag values can describe the nature of the node that has been reached in the traversal.

Let us now rewrite the generator shown as Prog. 1.4 with tags. The result is generator *preorderT* of Prog. 1.5. Here a natural choice for the tags additional to F is a set of values that indicate the successor structure of the node being returned, namely B(oth), L(eft), R(ight), or T(erminal), depending on whether the node has two children, just a left child, just a right child, or no children. All five values constitute the enumerated type tagtype. The meaning of the angular brackets in the generator heading is explained further down.

**generator** *preorderT*(*bin*: bintreetype; *null*: datumtype): <datumtype, tagtype>;

  **persistent** *stack*: stacktype; *node*: bintreetype;

  **temporary** *tag*: tagtype;

**begin**

  **if not** *emptytree*(*bin*) **then begin**

    *stack*:= *push*(*newstack, bin*);

    **while not** *emptytree*(*node*) **or not** *emptystack*(*stack*) **do begin**

      **if** *emptytree*(*node*) **then begin**

        *node*:= *read*(*stack*);  *stack*:= *pop*(*stack*)

      **end**;

      **if not** *emptytree*(*right*(*node*)) **then begin**

        *stack*:= *push*(*stack, right*(*node*));

        **if** *emptytree*(*left*(*node*)) **then** *tag*:= R

        **else** *tag*:= B

      **end**

      **else if** *emptytree*(*left*(*node*)) **then** *tag*:= T

      **else** *tag*:= L;

      **suspend** <*datum*(*node*), *tag*>;

      *node*:= *left*(*node*);

    **end**

  **end**;

  **while** true **do**

    **suspend** <*null*, F>

**end** (* *preorderT* *)

        Prog. 1.5 -- Preorder traversal with tagging

We now need to modify the usage conventions for generators. The generators of Progs. 1.1 - 1.4 are invoked just like functions. For example, if *pre* is an instance of the generator *preorder*, and the structure of the right-hand drawing of Fig. 1.2 is identified as a binary tree *bt*, then *pre(bt)* is given the values 25, 23, 22, 11, 19, 17 in the first six calls to *pre*.

Since generator *preorderT* returns two data items, and in principle a generator could return an arbitrarily long tuple of items, we propose a second usage mode for generators that is close to that of procedures. In this mode, a call to instance *preT* of generator *preorderT* takes the form

$$preT(bintree, -1) <D, T>$$

Here *bintree* indicates the binary tree that is to be traversed, and, after the first call to *preT*, *D* will hold the datum associated with the root of *bintree*, and *T* will hold its tag. After the second call these values will have been replaced by values associated with the node of *bintree* that comes second in the preorder traversal sequence.

The distinction in usage is reflected in the definition of a generator. If it is to have a "functional" usage, the heading of its definition takes the form

**generator** *name*(arguments): type-of-return;

If a "procedural" usage is intended, the heading takes the form

**generator** *name*(arguments): <type(s)-of-return(s)>;

Returning now to the problem of extracting a sentence from a parse tree, let us consider the parse tree of the sentence "the child ate a green pear," shown in Fig. 1.3.

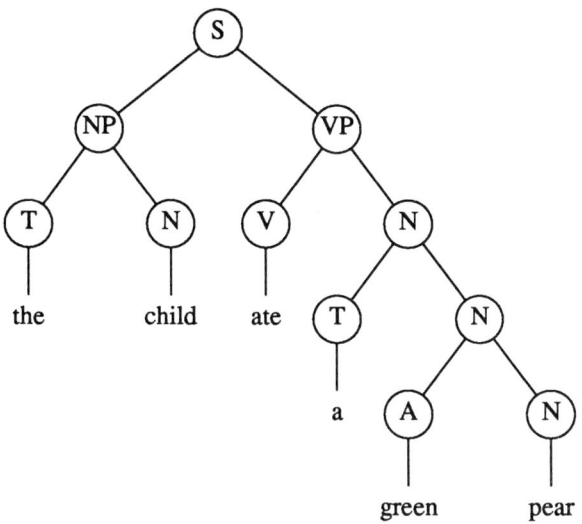

Fig. 1.3 -- A parse tree

Any traversal generator that identifies terminal nodes could be applied to a parse tree. However, a slight complication arises in that parse trees are not in general binary. Indeed, because the terminal nodes lack left or right orientation, the tree of Fig. 1.3 is not binary. But an arbitrary tree can be converted to a binary tree by means of the Knuth transformation: for every internal node $x$ in the tree, denote the nodes originating from $x$ in left to right order by $<x,y_1>$, $<x,y_2>$, ..., $<x,y_t>$; assign left orientation to arc $<x,y_1>$; replace the remaining arcs by arcs $<y_1,y_2>$, $<y_2,y_3>$, ..., $<y_{t-1},y_t>$, all with right orientation. For the tree of Fig. 1.3 the result is Fig. 1.4, where again the words of the sentence are terminal nodes.

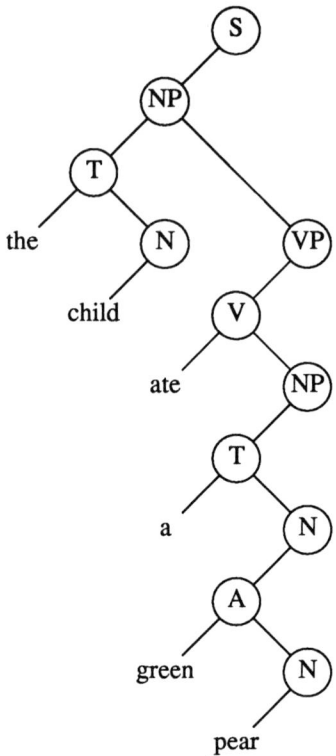

Fig. 1.4 -- Knuth transform of the tree of Fig. 1.3

Suppose that the binary tree of Fig. 1.4 is called *parsebin*, and that it is traversed by instance *preT* of generator *preorderT*. We want to collect the words of the sentence represented by *parsebin*. The code that now follows builds this sentence in an array *sentence*.

```
        index:= 0;
    repeat
        preT(parsebin, -1) <word, tag>;
        if tag = T then begin
            index:= index + 1;
            sentence[index]:= word
        end
    until tag = F
```

The use of the repeat-until is quite safe as long as the designer of a generator provides a do-forever loop into which to move after the generator has returned the last element of its sequence. Then the generator always returns something, even if it is only a null value. Let us examine this claim by considering an empty *parsebin*. Then in Prog. 1.5 an empty binary tree is assigned to *node*, and, since the boolean condition **not** *emptytree(node)* is false, control passes at once into the do-forever. Consequently a tag value of F is returned, the condition *tag* = T in our sentence generation code does not hold, and exit from the loop takes place with the array *sentence* empty.

## 1.5 THE VERIFICATION AND VALIDATION OBLIGATION

Every software developer is under an obligation to verify and validate all software released for use by others or used in ways that affect others. Since generators tend to fall into this category, verification and validation is an important part of programming with generators.

The development of a piece of software starts with the conception in someone's mind of what the software is to accomplish. When the initial idea has become sufficiently definite to be written down or otherwise communicated to the outside world, it becomes a requirements statement. The requirements statement should give rise to a formal specification of the software, and the software is then implemented in accordance with the formal specification. Verification is the determination that the software corresponds to its specification; validation is the determination that the specification corresponds to the requirements.

As an example we consider plateaus. Given an array of integers $A[1..n]$, a plateau is a contiguous sequence of at least two elements of $A$ that are all equal, and this sequence is bounded by elements that differ from the elements in the sequence, or by the beginning or end of the array. Thus, the array

| 7 | 5 | 6 | 6 | 6 | 6 | 8 | 3 | 3 |
|---|---|---|---|---|---|---|---|---|

contains a plateau of 4 elements starting in location 3, and a plateau of 2 elements starting in location 8. We want a program that returns the starting positions of all plateaus in a given array.

The above expresses requirements. The formal specification in this instance is relatively easy to write: given array $A[1..n]$, find the set
$$\{k \mid k \in 1..n-1 \wedge A[k] = A[k+1] \wedge k > 1 \longrightarrow A[k] \neq A[k-1]\}.$$
The development of the corresponding program should not be difficult either.

Verification takes three forms. The strongest is logical proof. For the plateau example we have a logical expression in $k$, and a $k$ is to become part of the result if and only if the logical expression is true for it. A logical proof establishes that the program does indeed put a $k$ into the output set if and only if the logical expression is true for it. This is done by a sequence of steps, where each step is the application of an inference rule of the logical system.

To take another example, for sorting one shows that the output is indeed sorted, and that the output is a permutation of the input. Specifications come in general in two parts: the first is a description of the required output, the second relates the output to the input, as in (1.7a) and (1.7b) below. It is generally harder to write the second part, and this part may also be the more difficult to prove.

$$\forall i: 0 < i < n: B[i] \leq B[i+1]; \tag{1.7a}$$

$$size(B) = size(A) \land \forall k: 1 \leq k \leq n:$$
$$card(\{ (A(k) = A(i)) = true \mid 1 \leq i \leq n \}) =$$
$$card(\{ (A(k) = B(i)) = true \mid 1 \leq i \leq n \}). \tag{1.7b}$$

Here (1.7a) states that array $B[1 .. n]$ is sorted in ascending order. Expression (1.7b) indicates that array $B$ is a permutation of array $A$ by stating that both arrays have the same number of elements and that every value found in $A$ must be replicated the same number of times in $A$ and $B$. This is done by counting equality statements -- $card$ returns the cardinality of a set, here a set of true statements.

Next is mathematical proof for which it is no longer required that each step of the proof be formally justified. Now it is not essential to have a formal specification -- a mathematical proof can take an informal requirements statement for its starting point. The weakest form of verification is testing, which is statistical in nature. In testing, we compare outputs of a program against our expectations based on the requirements statement (or a formal specification). The data gathered during testing can be interpreted in terms of a reliability model, and a predication made of the software failure rate for the future, that is, of the expected number of failures over a given period of time.

The progression of logical to mathematical to statistical is not necessarily a downward progression, and each form of verification has its uses. A formal proof can be used when a formal specification is relatively easy to write and to understand. However, all that the formal proof guarantees is consistency between program and specification.

When the specification is not easy to understand, then it is not unlikely that the specification is faulty, and the program, if consistent with the specification, will contain all the faults of the latter. In some cases, as we shall see in Chapter 2, the formal specification is too complicated for a logical proof to be practicable.

Mathematical arguments are problematic in that they can be in error. On the other hand, they take much less effort than logical proofs, and they can be applied in situations in which logical proofs are impracticable. The main problem with mathematical proofs is their possible incompleteness. For example, the proof may neglect to consider what happens with null input.

Some purists would not consider testing a part of verification. Their argument is that testing can merely show the presence of software faults -- that is, it cannot guarantee the absence of faults. This is, of course, a valid argument. However, with a large software system, although it may be feasible to establish the correctness of subcomponents of the system, either by logical proof or mathematical argument, proving is not feasible for the system as a whole.

Tests are particularly important in validation. Since a requirements statement is necessarily informal, there can be no formal proof of consistency between it and a formal specification. This leaves mathematical arguments and tests. But, as we pointed out above, a mathematical argument can be faulty or incomplete. Also, the interpretation of the requirements statement by the software developer may differ markedly from the intentions of its writer. Only the examination of the outputs of a program by the writer of the requirements statement can expose the misinterpretation.

A particularly good way of ensuring consistency of a program with a requirements statement is to write the requirements statement as a high-level program, and to transform this program, which may not even be executable in its initial form, into an efficient implementation by means of transformations. Again there is a formal approach and an informal one.

Under the formal approach one first proves for a library of transformations that all the transformations in the library preserve the input-output relation of a program, that is, one establishes that they are correctness preserving, and only members of the library are then allowed to be used in the transformation of a program. This has the advantage that the initial and final programs are guaranteed to be consistent. Unfortunately, with programs that solve real life problems, the right transformations are often not to be found in the library. Also, the transformational development consists of many small steps, which makes it difficult to pick out the right transformation for a given situation.

It would be convenient to automate the process of transformation, that is, to consider a specification such as (1.7a-1.7b) as an initial program. The specification then not only defines a goal to achieve, but is regarded as a means of achieving the goal. Although some programming languages can be regarded as first attempts at exploring ways of converting declarative specifications into more or less efficient code -- Prolog is perhaps the best-known example -- it is safe to say that "program" (1.7a-1.7b) is written in a language for which no compiler as yet exists, and that it will take a long time to develop such a compiler.

Under the informal approach one examines the structure of a program, and endeavours to cut down on unnecessary work by the program. Instead of making a series of small changes, as one would under the formal approach, a program may be transformed beyond recognition in a single step. The justification of a transformation is established by mathematical reasoning. Since the reasoning can be faulty, particularly for later versions of the program, in which clarity may have been traded for execution efficiency, it is not always good policy to try and achieve optimal execution efficiency. The risk of introducing faults in the program by so doing may be too great.

In this book we shall not deal with formal proofs or with tests. But we shall sometimes reason about the appropriateness of this or that step in the development of a program.

## 1.6 DEVELOPMENT OF A GENERATOR FOR PREORDER TRAVERSAL

Some generators find application in many different contexts -- they are basic building blocks of software. It is essential that such generators be dependable, and their dependability has to be established by verification.

Specifications such as that of (1.7a-1.7b) can be very difficult to write, and proofs are often hard and tedious. Program development by transformations is an approach to verification that bypasses some of these difficulties. Under transformational development a high-level "program" is one's starting point, where the quotes are used because this "program" need not be executable. This initial version is gradually transformed into a program that is not only executable but also efficient. One particularly pleasant aspect of this approach is that input-output correspondences are for the most part easily established. As regards sorting, one simply checks that no strange data are being picked up or any input data destroyed.

Let us apply this approach to the development of a generator for preorder traversal of a binary tree. In this case we shall start with a recursive procedure that is executable, but not necessarily efficient, and convert it into an efficient generator. The approach is based on the assumption that this initial version is so clear that its correctness is obvious, or, in other words, that it is a specification for the more refined transforms. Libraries of correctness-preserving transformations have been developed, and the mechanical application of such transformations guarantees that the resulting transforms are equivalent to the programs from which they derive, but, for the reasons pointed out in Section 1.5, we shall approach the transformation process informally here, depending on informal arguments to demonstrate the equivalence of successive versions of the traversal procedure. The initial recursive procedure for preorder traversal is Prog. 1.6. The *dealwith* of *pretraverse1* is a procedure that processes the data associated with the nodes of the binary tree. For example, *dealwith* may simply output the data.

    **procedure** *pretraverse1(bin*: bintreetype);

    **begin**

        **if not** *emptytree(bin)* **then begin**

            *dealwith(datum(bin))*;

            *pretraverse1(left(bin))*;

            *pretraverse1(right(bin))*

        **end**

    **end** (* *pretraverse1* *)

Prog. 1.6 -- A recursive specification of preorder traversal

The first transformation will eliminate calls to *pretraverse1* with empty binary trees as arguments. However, we will still have to determine whether or not the binary tree initially submitted to the procedure is empty. We use a construction under which the determination is made just once, in the non-recursive procedure *pretraverse2* of Prog. 1.7 that calls the embedded recursive procedure *recurse*.

The next step is to convert *pretraverse2* into a non-recursive procedure by introducing a stack, and replacing each call to *recurse* by a push operation. In addition, a while loop has to be introduced with an appropriate stopping criterion, and the argument of *dealwith* brought into accord with the other changes. The result is Prog. 1.8.

**procedure** *pretraverse2(bin:* bintreetype);

  **procedure** *recurse(bin:* bintreetype);

  **begin**

    *dealwith(datum(bin));*

    **if not** *emptytree(left(bin))* **then** *recurse(left(bin));*

    **if not** *emptytree(right(bin))* **then** *recurse(right(bin))*

  **end;** (* *recurse* *)

**begin**

  **if not** *emptytree(bin)* **then** *recurse(bin)*

**end** (* *pretraverse2* *)

        Prog. 1.7 -- Procedure *pretraverse1* transformed

**procedure** *pretraverse3(bin:* bintreetype); **var** *stack:* stacktype; *node:* bintreetype;
**begin**

  **if not** *emptytree(bin)* **then begin**

    *stack:= push(newstack, bin);*

    **while not** *emptystack(stack)* **do begin**

      *node:= read(stack); stack:= pop(stack);*

      *dealwith(datum(node));*

      **if not** *emptytree(right(node))* **then** *stack:= push(stack, right(node));*

      **if not** *emptytree(left(node))* **then** *stack:= push(stack, left(node))*

    **end**

  **end**

**end** (* *pretraverse3* *)

        Prog. 1.8 -- A nonrecursive procedure for preorder traversal

The analysis of the transition from *pretraverse2* to *pretraverse3* should be approached in a suspicious frame of mind. One should convince oneself positively that nothing has gone wrong. Two aspects need to be looked at in some detail: (a) the order in which the nodes of *bin* are processed by *dealwith*, and (b) the stopping criterion for the loop. According to *pretraverse1*, which is our specification, for any node of *bin*, the processing of this node is to be followed by the processing of first the left and then the right subtree of the node. Because the right subtree of a node is pushed down before the left subtree, the left subtree will be popped up first, and the required order of processing of the nodes is maintained. It is quite clear that every node ends up on the stack precisely once, so that emptiness of the stack indicates correctly the completion of the traversal.

We observe in *pretraverse3* that whenever a left subtree is pushed into the stack, it is immediately popped up again. The same holds for the root node of the entire binary tree. We should remove the redundant push/pop sequences, but when the sequences are removed, stack emptiness is no longer an adequate termination condition for the loop. Comparison of the statement

**if not** *emptytree(left(node))* **then** *stack:= push(stack, left(node))*

and its counterpart

**if not** *emptytree(left(node))* **then** *node:= left(node)*

suggests that the loop should terminate if the assignment to *node* is not made, and there is nothing in the stack. But how can we tell whether the assignment is or is not made? The best solution is to carry out the assignment in any case, and to test *node* for emptiness. Prog. 1.9 is the result.

**procedure** *pretraverse4*(*bin*: bintreetype);
    **var** *stack*: stacktype; *node*: bintreetype;
**begin**
    **if not** *emptytree*(*bin*) **then begin**
        *stack*:= *push*(*newstack*, *bin*);
        **while not** *emptytree*(*node*) **or not** *emptystack*(*stack*) **do begin**
            **if** *emptytree*(*node*) **then begin**
                *node*:= *read*(*stack*);  *stack*:= *pop*(*stack*)
            **end**;
            *dealwith*(*datum*(*node*));
            **if not** *emptytree*(*right*(*node*)) **then** *stack*:= *push*(*stack*, *right*(*node*));
            *node*:= *left*(*node*)
        **end**
    **end**
**end** (* *pretraverse4* *)

    Prog. 1.9 -- An improved procedure for preorder traversal

All that now remains is to include the final do-forever loop and make the other changes that convert the procedure into a generator. Such changes include the substitution of a suspend statement for the call to *dealwith*. The result is Prog. 1.4. Now, however, one should have greater confidence in Prog. 1.4 than when it was first seen because the systematic manner of its development has been made explicit.

## 1.7 THE TOWERS OF HANOI

The next example is somewhat contrived. It is the Towers of Hanoi problem, which is a trivial game. Moreover, it would be hard to find a reason why it should be implemented as a generator rather than an ordinary procedure. On the other hand, the problem provides a good illustration of the conversion of a recursive procedure into a non-recursive generator. The game is played with three pegs and $n$ discs, where no two discs have the same diameter. Initially all the discs are located on a single peg (the source), and the objective of the game is to move them to another peg (the destination). Only one disc at a time may be moved. The hard part is a requirement that at no time may a disc be located on top of another disc of smaller diameter. The initial configuration for a game with 5 discs, and with the pegs numbered 1, 2, and 3, is shown in Fig. 1.5.

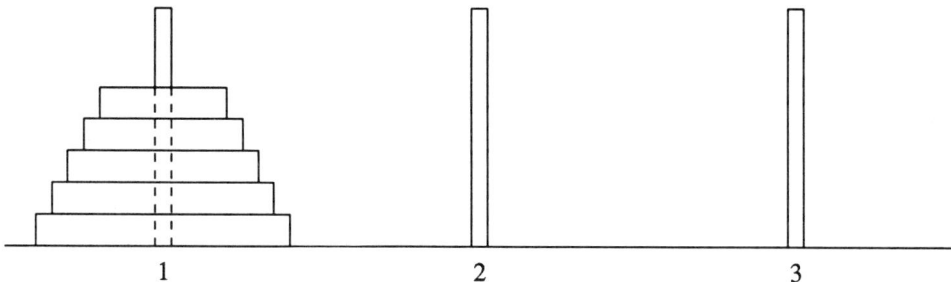

Fig. 1.5 -- The Towers of Hanoi game

The recursive solution is straightforward. In order to move five discs from peg 1 to peg 3 one should first move four discs from peg 1 to the spare peg 2 in an unspecified manner, then move the remaining disc from 1 to 3, and finally move the four discs from spare peg 2 to destination 3, again in an unspecified manner. The only problem with the recursive solution is the designation of the spare peg. However, when the pegs are identified by the numbers 1, 2, and 3, the sum of these identifiers is 6. Hence the identifier of the spare peg is (6 - *source* - *destination*). The recursive program is given as Prog. 1.10. The output generated by the call *hanoi1*(3, 1, 3), which is to move three discs from peg 1 to peg 3, would consist of the moves (1, 3), (1, 2), (3, 2), (1, 3), (2, 1), (2, 3), (1, 3).

**procedure** *hanoi1*(*n*: natural; *source, destination*: 1..3);
**begin**
   **if** $n > 0$ **then begin**
      *hanoi1*(*n* - 1, *source*, 6 - *source* - *destination*);
      *output*(*source, destination*);
      *hanoi1*(*n* - 1, 6 - *source* - *destination*, *destination*)
   **end**
**end** (* *hanoi1* *)

Prog. 1.10 -- A recursive procedure for the Towers of Hanoi game

An obvious way of making Prog. 1.10 more efficient is to remove calls with $n = 0$ (this halves the number of calls). The calls with $n = 0$ are removed by making a special case of $n = 1$ -- when $n = 1$, we just make a call to *output*. But then this can be made the only place at which calls to *output* are made: the reference to *output* in Prog. 1.10 can be replaced by another call to *hanoi1*, with $n = 1$. This will simplify the conversion to a generator later on. An initial test for $n = 0$ is still needed, and, just as was done with *pre-traverse2*, we embed the transformed recursive procedure into an outer procedure that merely performs this test. The result of all these changes is *hanoi2* of Prog. 1.11.

```
procedure hanoi2(n: natural; source, destination: 1..3);
    procedure towers(n: natural; source, destination: 1..3);
    begin
        if n = 1 then
            output(source, destination)
        else begin
            towers(n - 1, source, 6 - source - destination);
            towers(1, source, destination);
            towers(n - 1, 6 - source - destination, destination)
        end
    end; (* towers *)
begin
    if n > 0 then
        towers(n, source, destination)
end (* hanoi2 *)
```

Prog. 1.11 -- Improved recursive procedure for Towers of Hanoi

In the transformation of procedure *hanoi2* to a generator each recursive call needs to be replaced by an action that saves three items, namely the number of discs to be moved, their source, and their destination. Two options are open -- the three items can be assembled into a record, and the record pushed down on a stack, or three stacks can be used, one for each category of data. The second alternative is chosen for the generator of Prog. 1.12. Further optimization of the generator is left to the reader.

**generator** *hanoi*(*n*: natural; *source, destination*: 1..3): <1..3, 1..3>;
  **persistent** *sizestack, sourcestack, destinationstack*: stacktype;
  **temporary** *size*: natural; *from, to*: 1..3;
**begin**
  **if** *n* > 0 **then begin**
    *sizestack*:= *push(newstack, n)*;
    *sourcestack*:= *push(newstack, source)*;
    *destinationstack*:= *push(newstack, destination)*;
    **while not** *emptystack(sizestack)* **do begin**
      *size*:= *read(sizestack)*; *sizestack*:= *pop(sizestack)*;
      *from*:= *read(sourcestack)*; *sourcestack*:= *pop(sourcestack)*;
      *to*:= *read(destinationstack)*; *destinationstack*:= *pop(destinationstack)*;
      **if** *size* = 1 **then**
        **suspend** <*from, to*>
      **else begin**
        *sizestack*:= *push(sizestack, size-1)*;
        *sourcestack*:= *push(sourcestack, 6-from-to)*;
        *destinationstack*:= *push(destinationstack, to)*;
        *sizestack*:= *push(sizestack, 1)*;
        *sourcestack*:= *push(sourcestack, from)*;
        *destinationstack*:= *push(destinationstack, to)*;
        *sizestack*:= *push(sizestack, size-1)*;
        *sourcestack*:= *push(sourcestack, from)*;
        *destinationstack*:= *push(destinationstack, 6-from-to)*
      **end**
  **end**

                **end**;

            **while** true **do**

                **suspend** <0, 0>

    **end** (* *hanoi* *)

        Prog. 1.12 -- Move generator for the Towers of Hanoi game

## 1.8 A STUDY OF INORDER TRAVERSAL

A procedure for inorder traversal of a binary tree is obtained by interchanging the first two statements in the body of the embedded procedure *recurse* of Prog. 1.7:

>  **if not** *emptytree(left(bin))* **then** *recurse(left(bin))*;
>
>  *dealwith(datum(bin))*;
>
>  **if not** *emptytree(right(bin))* **then** *recurse(right(bin))*

Similarly, a procedure for postorder traversal would be obtained by writing the statements of the body of *recurse* in the order

> **if not** *emptytree(left(bin))* **then** *recurse(left(bin))*;
>
> **if not** *emptytree(right(bin))* **then** *recurse(right(bin))*;
>
> *dealwith(datum(bin))*

The removal of recursion from Prog. 1.7 was easy because the nonrecursive part of the body of *recurse* comes before the recursive calls. It was also relatively easy in the transition from *hanoi2* (Prog. 1.11) to *hanoi* (Prog. 1.12) because the actual generation of a move arises if and only if $n = 1$. We note, however, a structural similarity between the procedure for inorder traversal defined above and *hanoi1* (Prog. 1.10). On the basis of this similarity we propose Prog. 1.13 -- we call it *intraverse2*, having reserved the name *intraverse1* for the adaptation of Prog. 1.7 to inorder traversal.

**procedure** *intraverse2*(*bin*: bintreetype);
  **procedure** *recurse*(*first*: boolean; *bin*: bintreetype);
  **begin**
    **if not** *first* **then**
      *dealwith*(*datum*(*bin*));
    **else begin**
      **if not** *emptytree*(*left*(*bin*)) **then** *recurse*(true, *left*(*bin*));
      *recurse*(false, *bin*);
      **if not** *emptytree*(*right*(*bin*)) **then** *recurse*(true, *right*(*bin*))
    **end**
  **end**; (* *recurse* *)
**begin**
  **if not** *emptytree*(*bin*) **then** *recurse*(true, *bin*)
**end** (* *intraverse2* *)

Prog. 1.13 -- Recursive inorder traversal

Still following the Towers of Hanoi analogy, *intraverse2* is converted into the generator *intraverse3* by providings two stacks, one for values of *first*, the other for subtrees that remain to be processed. Prog. 1.14 is the result, where we have left the introduction of tags and of the final do-forever loop to a more refined version of the generator.

**generator** *intraverse3*(*bin*: bintreetype): datumtype;
  **persistent** *switchstack*: boolstacktype; *nodestack*: bintreestacktype;
  **temporary** *first*: boolean; *node*: bintreetype;
**begin**
  **if not** *emptytree*(*bin*) **then begin**

*switchstack*:= *push(newstack,* true);

*nodestack*:= *push(newstack, bin)*;

**while not** *emptystack(nodestack)* **do begin**

    *first*:= *read(switchstack)*; *switchstack*:= *pop(switchstack)*;

    *node*:= *read(nodestack)*; *nodestack*:= *pop(nodestack)*;

    **if not** first **then**

        **suspend** <*datum(node)*>

    **else begin**

        **if not** *emptytree(right(node))* **then begin**

            *switchstack*:= *push(switchstack,* true);

            *nodestack*:= *push(nodestack, right(node))*

        **end**;

        *switchstack*:= *push(switchstack,* false);

        *nodestack*:= *push(nodestack, node)*;

        **if not** *emptytree(left(node))* **then begin**

            *switchstack*:= *push(switchstack,* true);

            *nodestack*:= *push(nodestack, left(node))*

        **end**

        **end**

    **end**

**end**

**end** (* *intraverse3* *)

Prog. 1.14 -- Tagless generator for inorder traversal

The analogy to the Towers of Hanoi program should not be carried too far.

Whereas *hanoi* of Prog. 1.12 has three arguments and uses three stacks, *intraverse3* has only one argument, but still uses two stacks. This suggests that *switchstack* has been introduced in Prog. 1.14 merely as a programming device, and we should now try and eliminate the need for it. Note, however, that we should aim at a higher level of efficiency only when the attainment of such efficiency is cost effective. If the inorder generator is not to be used very often, we should add tag assignment commands and the do-forever loop to Prog. 1.14, and then accept it as is. Any further refinement carries with it additional programming costs. Moreover, changes may introduce faults.

If we were to carry on, several possibilities for change suggest themselves. First, the initial test of *bin* for emptiness could be combined with the test of *nodestack* for emptiness. Second, some push/pop sequences could be eliminated. For example, if the left subtree of a node is not empty, then the subtree is pushed down to be popped up immediately afterwards, but, if it is empty, then the node itself is pushed down to be popped up immediately afterwards. Third, the circumstances under which the generation of a datum takes place should be analysed in some detail, where the aim is the elimination of *switchstack*. For the purposes of what follows we shall refer to nodes for which the corresponding value on *switchstack* is false as output nodes.

The pushing down of an output node can be followed by the pushing down of its left subtree, which is immediately popped up again, the pushing down of the right subtree of the root of this left subtree, the pushing down of the root of the left subtree as an output node, and so forth. In other words, two sequences of nodes get pushed down to stay in the node stack: roots of left subtrees, which are output nodes, and roots of right subtrees. Moreover, the root of a right subtree will be located in the node stack immediately below an output node of which this is the right subtree. Hence we need to push down the output nodes alone, and to access their right subtrees after the output nodes have been delivered up by the generator. Prog. 1.15, which is a complete inorder generator for binary trees, incorporates the changes discussed above.

    **generator** *inorderT(bin*: treetype; *null*: datumtype): <datumtype, tagtype>;

      **persistent** *stack*: stacktype; *node*: treetype;

      **temporary** *tag*: tagtype;

    **begin**

      *node*:= *bin*;

      *stack*:= *newstack*;

      **while not** *emptytree(node)* **or not** *emptystack(stack)* **do begin**

          **while not** *emptytree(node)* **do begin**

              *stack*:= *push(stack, node)*;

              *node*:= *left(node)*

          **end**;

          *node*:= *read(stack)*; *stack*:= *pop(stack)*;

          **if** *emptytree(left(node))* **then**

              **if** *emptytree(right(node))* **then** *tag*:= T

              **else** *tag*:= R

          **else if** *emptytree(right(node))* **then** *tag*:= L

          **else** *tag*:= B;

          **suspend** <*datum(node), tag*>;

          *node*:= *right(node)*

      **end**;

      **while true do**

          **suspend** <*null*, F>

    **end** (* *inorderT* *)

      Prog. 1.15 -- Generator for inorder traversal of binary trees

## 1.9 SUMMARY OF PROPERTIES OF GENERATORS

Generators produce the elements of a data sequence in a stream. The sequence can be computed by means of a formula, such as a recurrence relation, or it can be defined by a traversal discipline applied to a data-carrying device, such as an array or a binary tree.

Generators are an extension of functions. This is quite obvious in the case of a sequence defined by a formula. Although the calling mode for some generators resembles that of procedures, they are still more closely related to functions than to procedures in that any change to arguments passed as values is internal to the generator, that is, it affects only local copies of the arguments. Such arguments are passed into an instance of a generator just once, at the time of the first call to this instance. The reason why the call may have to resemble a procedure call is that a generator is some cases returns a vector of values. A procedure-like call facilitates access to components of the vector.

More than one instance of the same generator may be declared. These instances perform the actual generation. The definition of a generator consists of a heading, declarations, and a body. The first line is the heading, which takes one of the following forms:

> **generator** *name*(arguments): type-of-return-value;
>
> **generator** *name*(arguments): <type(s)-of-return-value(s)>;

The angular brackets indicate the usage mode of the generator. If they are absent, then the generator is called like a function, and it returns just a single entity. This entity is the value of the identifier of the instance of the generator being called. If the angular brackets are present, the generator is called in a procedural mode, and the return values are available until they are overwritten in the calling program or by a later call to the generator. Suppose we have the following two calls in sequence:

$$instancename(............) <Q, R>;$$

$$instancename(............) <X, Y>$$

Values identified by $Q, R, X$, and $Y$ are all available after the execution of the second call.

After the heading the generator definition contains variable declarations. A variable can be defined as either persistent or temporary. Persistent variables preserve their values between calls to the generator, and so do the local copies of the input arguments.

The generator body follows the declarations. It is to contain at least one suspend statement. Whenever execution of the generator code reaches a suspend statement, control is returned to the calling program and the values associated with the suspend statement become available to the calling program. If the generator definition indicates that it is to be called in the functional mode, the angular brackets following the "suspend" are to contain just one item. If the generator is to be called in a procedural mode, then these brackets may enclose more than one item. The objects enclosed by the angular brackets belonging to the generator heading, all suspend statements, and calls to all instances of this generator must agree in number and type.

When a generator instance is called for the first time, execution begins with the first statement of the generator body. In subsequent calls execution begins with the first statement that follows the "suspend" that terminated execution in the previous invocation of this generator instance. After the generator has returned its sequence of values, execution of the generator should become confined to a do-forever loop. Otherwise an exceptional (error) condition arises when the end of the generator body is reached. Of course, there are some limitations to the persistence of our generators. When used with a block-structured language, an instance of a generator becomes deactivated on exit from the block in which it has been declared.

# 2

# Application of Generators

The tag values introduced in Section 1.4 serve several purposes. First, for a generator that goes through a finite iteration sequence, an ultimate tag value of F (for Finished) indicates when generation of the sequence has been completed. Second, tag values help ensure full implementation independence. If one needs to know whether the node currently being accessed in a binary tree is terminal, say, the current tag value supplies this information. Third, tag values can be used in the specification of complicated programs that make use of several generators. Most of the examples discussed here illustrate various uses of tags.

## 2.1 INTERMESHED BINARY TREE TRAVERSALS

An algorithm for the strong components of a directed graph can be based on traversals of a tree representation of the directed graph. The algorithm has two intermeshed phases. In the first phase the tree is traversed under preorder, and numbers are allocated to the nodes of the tree. In the second phase the tree is traversed under postorder, and the allocated numbers are modified until all nodes that belong to the same strong component bear the same number. We shall call these processing steps A and B, respectively.

The algorithm starts out in the preorder phase. Whenever it is in the preorder phase it continues in this phase until a terminal node is reached. Postorder then takes over, and postorder traversal continues for as long as the nodes being reached have already been traversed under preorder. We shall use a Knuth transform of the general tree, and we need then to define traversals in this binary tree that are equivalent to preorder and postorder traversals of the general tree, as well as find characterizations of the nodes at which a switch from one to the other traversal takes place. Fig. 2.1 shows a general tree and its Knuth transform.

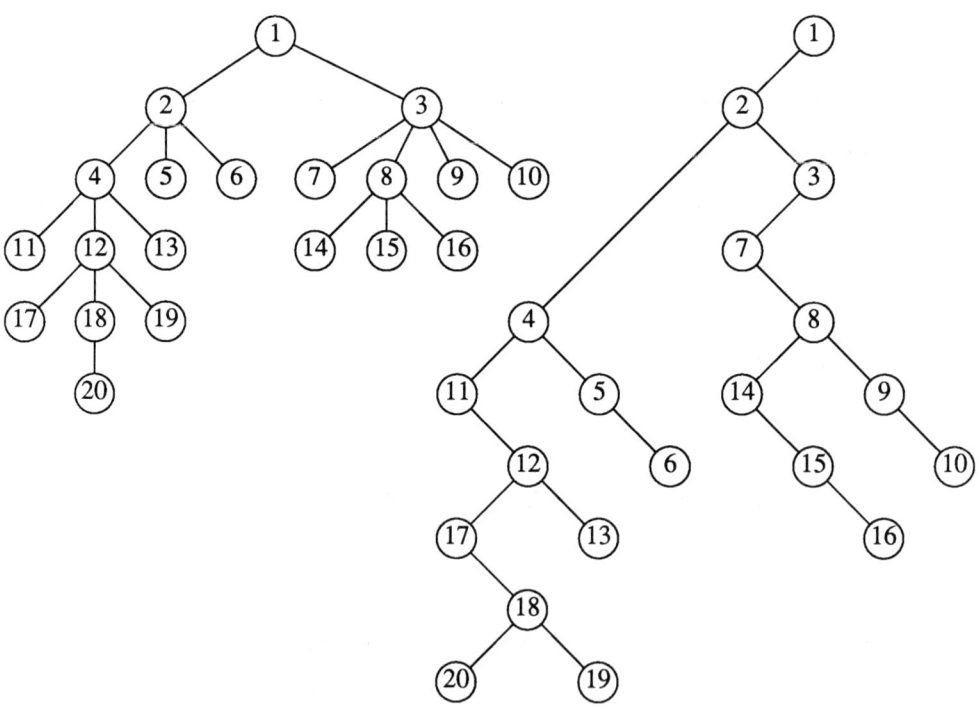

Fig. 2.1 -- A tree and its Knuth transform

Preorder and postorder traversal sequences for the general tree are, respectively,

1 2 4 11 12 17 18 20 19 13 5 6 3 7 8 14 15 16 9 10

11 17 20 18 19 12 13 4 5 6 2 7 14 15 16 8 9 10 3 1

Inspection of Fig. 2.1 shows that preorder traversal of the binary tree generates the same sequence as preorder traversal of the general tree from which it derives, but that postorder traversal of the general tree is equivalent to inorder traversal of the transform. The strong components algorithm thus becomes based on an intermeshing of preorder and inorder traversals of the Knuth transform. A node is a terminal node in the general tree if and only if the corresponding node in the transform has no left child. The cross-over points from inorder to preorder are defined by nodes that have right children. By the nature of the Knuth transformation, the root node of the transform has no right child. So the stopping criterion for the algorithm should be the completion of the inorder traversal. The "double traversal" is defined by the following sequence, in which the bold numbers and the italic numbers define the preorder and postorder phases, respectively:

**1 2 4 11** *11* **12 17** *17* **18 20** *20* 18 **19** *19* 12 **13** *13* **4 5** *5* **6** *6*

*2 3* **7** *7* **8 14** *14* **15** *15* **16** *16* 8 **9** *9* **10** *10 3 1*

The entire process is defined in a schematic manner by Prog. 2.1, where *preord* is an instance of generator *preorderT* (Prog. 1.5) or of a generator derived from Prog. 1.9, and *inord* an instance of *intraverseT* (Prog. 1.15).

>     **repeat**
>
>>     **repeat**
>>
>>>     *preord*(*knuthbin*, -1) <*prenode, pretag*>;
>>>
>>>     **if** *pretag* ≠ F **then**
>>>
>>>>     processing step A (see p. 53) applied to node *prenode*
>>>
>>>     **until** *pretag* = T **or** *pretag* = R **or** *pretag* = F;
>>
>>     **repeat**
>>
>>>     *inord*(*knuthbin*, -1) <*innode, intag*>;
>>>
>>>     **if** *intag* ≠ F **then**
>>>
>>>>     processing step B (see p. 53) applied to node *innode*
>>>
>>>     **until** *intag* = R **or** *intag* = B **or** *intag* = F
>
>     **until** *intag* = F

Prog. 2.1 -- Structure of a strong component algorithm

Let us now sketch a demonstration of the correctness of Prog. 2.1. First, if the input to the program is an empty binary tree, *pretag* ≠ F is false after the first call to *preord* and *intag* ≠ F is false after the first call to *inord*. Hence no processing is done. Second, note that the strong component algorithm applied to a nonempty *knuthbin* consists of an equal number of preorder and inorder phases. Let us consider just the last pair of these phases. Exit from the first inner loop occurs when the last terminal node of the original tree has been processed (it is also the last terminal node of *knuthbin*), and the process moves into the second inner loop. Normally exit from this loop takes place when *intag* = R or *intag* = B, which indicate that the reached node has a right child. However, in the last phase of *inord*, the root node of *knuthbin*, which is the last node to be processed, cannot have a right child (by the nature of the Knuth transformation). Hence *inord* is called one more time, *intag* receives the value F, processing step B is bypassed, and exit takes place from both the second inner loop and the outer loop.

## 2.2 A TEXT FORMATTER

Participants of the 4th International Workshop on Specification and Design in April of 1987 were expected to try out their approaches on one of four problems given to them in April of 1986. One of the problems was a text formatter, for which the English specification is as follows:

"Given a non-negative integer, MAXPOS, and a character set including two break characters, blank and newline. For a sequence of characters S, we define a *word* as a non-empty sequence of consecutive non-break characters embedded between break characters or the end points of S.

"The program should accept as input a finite sequence of characters and produce as output a sequence of characters satisfying the following conditions.

1-- If the input sequence contains MAXPOS+1 consecutive non-break characters then the output sequence consists of a blank.

2-- If the input sequence includes at least one break for any consecutive MAXPOS+1 characters, then

2.1-- All the words of the input appear in the output in the same order and the output has no word which does not appear in the input.

2.2-- Furthermore, the output must meet the following constraints:

2.2.1--

The output contains no leading or tailing breaks, nor does it have two consecutive breaks.

2.2.2--

Any MAXPOS+1 consecutive characters include a newline.

2.2.3--

Any subsequence of the output made up of no more than MAXPOS consecutive characters and embedded between the head of the output or a newline on the left and the tail of the output or a blank on the right does not contain a newline."

The specification shows up some of the problems with the writing of specifications in general, and the use of English in particular. First, the specification is incomplete in that it does not tell how to treat an input that is less than MAXPOS+1 characters long. In particular, what is to happen if all these characters are breaks? Second, what exactly does *embedded* in 2.2.3 mean?

Let us amplify the English specification, and introduce some definitions. We shall say that the input is a string over the alphabet CH, and that this string is to be split into lines. The input consists of words separated by sequences of blanks (BK) and newlines (NL). Let BC = {BK, NL}. Then a word is a sequence of characters from SC = CH - BC such that the character to the left of this sequence (if any) and the character to the right of the sequence (if any) belong to BC. The first word of the input may be preceded by characters from BC, and characters from BC may follow the last word of the input.

The output is to contain precisely the words of the input in precisely the order that they have in the input. The length of an output line is not to exceed the value MAXPOS. If the input contains a word that consists of more than MAXPOS characters, then the entire output is to be just the one single character BK. The first word of the output is not to be preceded by any characters from BC, and the last word is not to be followed by any such characters. The objective is to minimize the number of output lines. This objective is achieved if the output lines are built up in the order they have in the output, and for every line an attempt is made to pack as much of the remaining input into this line as the line can take. We shall express these requirements formally, as a set of predicates. Denote a string by $S(1)S(2)...S(N)$, where $Length(S) = N$. Then let the input string be $B(1)B(2)...B(Length(B))$, and the output string $C(1)C(2)...C(Length(C))$. There are two parts to the specification. The first part consists of predicates that we consider of sufficiently general interest to be part of the data type of strings of words. The other part consists of predicates specific to this application.

Three predicates are to belong to the data type of strings of words: $Word(S, i, j)$ is true if the character sequence $S(i)...S(j)$ defines a word; $WordNumber(S, k, i, j)$ is true if $S(i)...S(j)$ defines the $k$th word of $S$; $WordCount(S, k)$ is true if $S$ contains $k$ words.

$Word(S: \text{string}; i, j: 1..Length(S)) =$
    $i \leq j$
    $\wedge \ (i \neq 1) \longrightarrow S(i-1) \in BC$
    $\wedge \ (j \neq Length(S)) \longrightarrow S(j+1) \in BC$
    $\wedge \ \forall \ k: i \leq k \leq j: (S(k) \in SC)$.

$WordNumber(S: \text{string}; k, i, j: \text{cardinal}) =$
    $Word(S, i, j)$
    $\wedge \ (k = 1) \longrightarrow \forall \ t: 1 \leq t < i: (S(t) \in BC)$
    $\wedge \ (k > 1) \longrightarrow \exists \ u, v: u, v \in \text{cardinal}: (WordNumber(S, k-1, u, v) \wedge$
                  $\forall \ t: v < t < i: (S(t) \in BC))$.

$WordCount(S: \text{string}; k: \text{natural}) =$
    $(k = 0) \longrightarrow \forall \ t: 1 \leq t \leq Length(S): (S(t) \in BC)$
    $\wedge \ (k > 0) \longrightarrow \exists \ u, v: u, v \in \text{cardinal}: (WordNumber(S, k, u, v) \wedge$
                  $\forall \ t: v < t \leq Length(S): (S(t) \in BC))$.

Let us examine the predicate *Word* in some detail. The four conjuncts in its definition establish, respectively, that limits $i$ and $j$ are properly related, that $S(i)...S(j)$

either starts at the left boundary of $S$ or has a break preceding it, that $S(i)...S(j)$ either ends at the right boundary of $S$ or has a break following it, and that no characters in $S(i)...S(j)$ are breaks. In the definition of *WordNumber* the first conjunct identifies the character sequence defined by $i$ and $j$ as a word. Then it is asserted that all characters preceding the first word are breaks. Suppose there are no such characters. Then $i = 1$, and no $t$ can satisfy the range condition $1 \le t < i$. That is, the quantification is over an empty set, but an important property of quantifiers is that a universally quantified expression over an empty set is always true (the corresponding existentially quantified expression is always false). The sequence number of subsequent words is established recursively: it is asserted that there exist character positions $u$ and $v$ that define word $k\text{-}1$, and that all characters between the end of this word and word $k$ are breaks. The interpretation of the definition of *WordCount* is left as an exercise.

The next set of predicates relates to the application. Predicate *Agrees* matches up the output words with the input words, and predicate *SpecialCase* determines whether or not the input contains any word that is too long. Predicates *BreaksOk* and *LinesOk* relate to the output: *BreaksOk* establishes that there are no leading or trailing breaks, and that there is precisely one break between each pair of words; *LinesOk* establishes the proper placement of newlines.

*Agrees* ($B$, $C$: string) =
  $\exists\, k\colon k \in$ natural: (*WordCount* ($B$, $k$) $\wedge$ *WordCount* ($C$, $k$) $\wedge$
  $\forall\, t\colon 1 \le t \le k\colon$ ($\exists\, i, j, u, v\colon i, j, u, v \in$ cardinal:
    (*WordNumber* ($B$, $t$, $i$, $j$) $\wedge$ *WordNumber* ($C$, $t$, $u$, $v$) $\wedge$
    $j - i = v - u$ $\wedge$
    $\forall\, q\colon 0 \le q \le j - i\colon$ ($B\,(i + q) = C\,(u + q)$))))).

*SpecialCase* ($B$: string) =
  $\exists\, i, j\colon 1 \le i < j \le Length\,(B)\colon$ (*Word* ($B$, $i$, $j$) $\wedge$ $j - i \ge$ MAXPOS).

$BreaksOk\,(C:\text{string}) = Length\,(C) > 0 \rightarrow$
$\quad C(1) \notin BC$
$\quad \wedge\ C(Length\,(C)) \notin BC$
$\quad \wedge\ \forall\ j:\ 1 < j < Length\,(C):\ (C(j) \in BC \rightarrow C(j+1) \notin BC).$

$LinesOk\,(C:\text{string}) =$
$\quad (\forall\ i:\ 1 < i < Length\,(C):\ (C(i) \neq NL)) \rightarrow Length\,(C) \leq MAXPOS$
$\quad \wedge$
$\quad \forall\ i:\ 1 < i < Length\,(C):\ (C(i) = NL \rightarrow$
$\qquad (Length\,(C) - i \leq MAXPOS\ \vee\ \exists\ j:\ i < j \leq MAXPOS + i + 1:\ (C(j) = NL)$
$\qquad \wedge$
$\qquad \exists\ k:\ i < k \leq Length\,(C):\ (Word\,(C, i+1, k)$
$\qquad\quad \wedge\ i+1 \leq MAXPOS\ \rightarrow\ k > MAXPOS$
$\qquad\quad \wedge\ i+1 > MAXPOS\ \rightarrow$
$\qquad\qquad \exists\ q:\ i - MAXPOS - 1 < q < i:\ (C(q) = NL\ \wedge$
$\qquad\qquad i+1 \leq q + MAXPOS\ \rightarrow k > q + MAXPOS)))).$

$ConversionOk\,(B, C:\text{string}) =$
$\quad SpecialCase\,(B) \rightarrow (Length\,(C) = 1 \wedge C(1) = BK)$
$\quad \wedge\ not(SpecialCase\,(B)) \rightarrow (Agrees\,(B, C) \wedge BreaksOk\,(C) \wedge LinesOk\,(C));$

Predicate *Agrees* asserts that strings B and C contain the same number of words, that corresponding words in B and C contain the same number of characters, and that corresponding characters in these words are equal.

The definition of *LinesOk* is the most difficult to interpret. Let us examine it line by line. The second line states that if the output string contains no newlines, then its length may not exceed MAXPOS. The rest of the specification deals with each NL in turn, the NL being specified as the C(i) in line 4. Line 5 establishes that either the end of the string or another NL is not too far away from C(i) on its right. This corresponds to requirement 2.2.2 in the original specification. Lines 7-11 deal with requirement 2.2.3. Line 7 picks out the word that follows C(i). In line 8 a special case is made of the first line of the output. Here the beginning of the string provides a reference point, and the word that follows $C(i)$ is tested against the limit MAXPOS: if the word starts on or to the left of the limit, then it must end to the right of the limit. For subsequent output lines the reference point is the nearest NL to the left of $C(i)$. Its location is established as $q$ in line 10, and line 11 is an analogue of line 8.

The specification of the text formatter was difficult to write, and it is difficult to interpret. So one has to ask what purpose it serves. Generally a specification has three purposes. First, it expresses the requirements of a client in an unambiguous manner. Second, it defines a high level reference for the software developer. Third, it is the reference point against which an implementation is to be verified. Unfortunately our predicative specification of the text formatter does not serve any of these purposes.

As a statement of requirements it fails because the client capable of writing the predicative specification as shown here should be capable of writing the corresponding program in much less time. I suspect that the writing of the specification as statements in English also took more time than it would have taken to write the program.

Moreover, I am not confident even now, after the specification has been scrutinized over a long period of time, that it expresses the requirements properly. One of the most frequent programming errors is a loop count off by one. Can we confidently say that the quantification range for $q$ in the last line of the definition of *Agrees* is what it should be? What about the inequalities in lines 10 and 11 of the definition of *LinesOk*? Actually, the definition of *Agrees* did not originally contain line 5. This fault was discovered only after many people had already studied the specification.

The point here is that the specification is so difficult to understand that faults can remain undiscovered for a long time. In contrast to recursive specifications Progs. 1.6 and 1.10, which clearly indicate what the program is to accomplish, the opacity of the predicates in the specification of the formatter makes this specification unsuitable as a starting point for program development.

There is much to be said for developing a formal specification and a program independently, and checking the two for consistency. This is program proving, which can show up faults in both specification and program. However, I see no way in which a formal proof of a program based on this specification could be produced in reasonable time.

Our example suggests that there are instances in which the best specification of a program is the program itself. However, the program must then be very transparent in the indication of its purpose. The use of generators can assist in attaining the transparency. In the formatter example, a generator can deliver the words of the input one by one. Thus the details of how the input is separated into words is removed from the program that assembles these words into the output text. The output is assembled by Prog. 2.2, which receives its input from generator *getword*. The generator returns a word (as an array of characters) and its length. When the input text has become exhausted, the length value returned by *getword* is zero. If the input contains no words, the length value is zero after the first call.

*index*:= 0;

*linelength*:= 0;

**repeat**

    *getword*(*string*) <*word, length*>;

    **if** *length* > 0 **then begin**

        **if** *length* > MAXPOS **then begin** (* special case *)

            *outstring*[1]:= BK;

            *index*:= 1;

    **end**

    **else begin**

        **if** *index* > 0 **then begin** (* insertion of break character *)

            *index*:= *index* + 1

            **if** *linelength*+1+*length* ≤ MAXPOS **then begin**

                *outstring*[*index*]:= BK;

                *linelength*:= *linelength* + 1 + *length*

            **end**

            **else begin**

                *outstring*[*index*]:= NL;

                *linelength*:= *length*

            **end**

        **end**

        **else**

            *linelength*:= *length*;

        **for** *i*:= 1 **to** *length* **do begin** (* transfer of word *)

            *index*:= *index* + 1;

            *outstring*[*index*]:= *word*[*i*]

                end

            end

        end

    **until** *length*=0 **or** *length*>MAXPOS

Prog. 2.2 -- A text formatting program

An informal demonstration of the correctness of Prog. 2.2 with respect to the requirements stated at the start of this section is now quite easy. There are these points to watch:

a. An empty input results in empty output.

b. When the length of a word exceeds MAXPOS, the output is a single blank.

c. If no input word is longer than MAXPOS, every input word is transferred to the output precisely once.

d. There are no leading or tailing breaks in the output.

e. The breaks are properly placed in the output.

f. The program terminates properly.

Let us consider the points in turn. (a) When the input is empty, the first call to *getword* sets *length* equal to 0, the processing section of the loop is not entered, and exit from the loop takes place with *getword* = 0, as required. (b) The processing section of the loop begins with a test on the length of a word, and every word is tested until the exit from the loop takes place. If the length of a word exceeds MAXPOS, the first character of the output becomes a blank, the length of the output is set to 1, and an exit from the loop takes place, again as required. (c) Every iteration of the loop results in a call to *getword*, and unless the length of the word delivered by *getword* is zero or greater than

MAXPOS, all the characters of the word are transferred to *outstring* in contiguous locations. Since the transfer is followed at once by another call to *getword*, a word cannot be transferred more than once. (d) After a word with length between 1 and MAXPOS has been delivered, an appropriate break is inserted *before* the word. This ensures that there will be no tailing break. The section that inserts breaks is bypassed when *index* = 0, which means that no leading break is inserted. (e) The section that inserts breaks is entered with *index* still indicating the position of the last character of the previous word in *outstring*. The incrementation of *index* before anything else will result in the proper placement of the break. The quantity *linelength* + 1 + *length* is made up of the length of the line already assembled, the length of the current word, and allowance for the break that is to come between the two. If this quantity does not exceed MAXPOS, the break is BK and we continue in the current line; otherwise it is NL, and, since the current word then starts a new line, the length of this word is the new value of *linelength*. Consider what happens when *linelength* + 1 + *length* = MAXPOS. Then a blank is inserted before the current word, and, although we could insert NL after this word, we postpone the insertion until after the next call to *getword*. If this call returns a word of zero length, nothing needs to be done. Otherwise the NL will now be inserted between the old and the new words. (f) Abnormal termination has already been considered under (a) and (b). In the normal case the last word of the input is transferred to the output, the next call to *getword* results in *length* = 0, and exit from the loop takes place with *index* referring to the last character of the last word of the text.

## 2.3 SORTING AND THE TWO-WAY MERGE

A key concept in sorting is a *run*. Let us define a run of keys in terms of a key sequence represented by the array $Q[1..n]$. Predicate *Run* is true if elements $i$ to $j$

(inclusive) of $Q$ form a run:

$$Run(Q,i,j) = i \leq j \land \forall k: i \leq k < j : (Q[k] \leq Q[k+1])$$
$$\land\ i > 1 \rightarrow Q[i] < Q[i-1]$$
$$\land\ j < n \rightarrow Q[j] > Q[j+1];$$

Consider input streams of records defined by the following key sequences.

A: 5 7 3 12 57 32 17 19 27 18 43 15

B: 2 9 11 8 15 30 42 20 35

Runs from the input streams are merged to produce output runs. Thus (5,7) and (2,9,11) yield (2,5,7,9,11); (3,12,57) and (8,15,30,42) yield (3,8,12,15,30,42,57); (32) and (20,35) yield (20,32,35). The merged runs are shunted alternately to output streams $C$ and $D$. At this point input stream $B$ has been exhausted, but three runs still remain in stream $A$. The first and third go to $D$, the second to $C$. The output streams are

C: 2 5 7 9 11 20 32 35 18 43

D: 3 8 12 15 30 42 57 17 19 27 15

Note here that (2, 5, 7, 9, 11) and (20, 32, 35) derive from different sets of input runs, but that they have coalesced into a single output run. The merging action that we have just performed is known as two-way merge, and it is the basis for merge sorting, a popular method for sorting large files. The next pass of merge sort would be another two-way merge in runs from $C$ and $D$ are merged back to $A$ and $B$, with the result

A: 2 3 5 7 8 9 11 12 15 20 30 32 35 42 57 15

B: 17 18 19 27 43

Now we have two runs on $A$ and one, consisting of a single key, on $B$. Next all the keys except the second 15 from $A$ will be merged onto $C$, and the 15 will go onto $D$. One last pass will then produce a sorted output on $A$. Normally, of course, the runs would consist of records rather than just keys. However, the essence of the method and of the programs to follow is brought out in a clearer fashion if we assume that the "records" consist of keys alone.

We have already defined the predicate *Run*. In analogy to the text formatter of the preceding section we could define predicates *RunNumber* and *RunCount*, and from them construct a predicative specification of two-way merge. However, such a specification makes even less sense here because two-way merge provides an ideal example of rigorous program development in terms of generators.

We require a generator that delivers the next value of a data stream, and associates a tag with the value. There are to be three tag values: N(ormal), H(old), and F(inished). The value H is to be associated with the last element of a run, unless this is the last element of the entire input stream, in which case the value is to be F. Otherwise it is to be N. In terms of the input stream

$$5 \ 7 \ 3 \ 12 \ 57 \ 32 \ 17 \ 19 \ 27 \ 18 \ 43 \ 15$$

the sequence of returns by the generator is to be

<5, N>, <7, N>, <7, H>,

<3, N>, <12, N>, <57, N>, <57, H>,

<32, N>, <32, H>,

<17, N>, <19, N>, <27, N>, <27, H>,

<18, N>, <43, N>, <43, H>,

<15, N>, <15, F>.

Every subsequent call is to return <15, F>. We could just as easily design a generator that has the sequence of returns

<5, N>, <7, H>,

<3, N>, <12, N>, <57, H>,

<32, H>,

<17, N>, <19, N>, <27, H>,

<18, N>, <43, H>,

<15, N>, <15, F>.

However, this generator would not be as effective for dealing with the two-way merge problem.

Let us now assume that the generator has state, defined by the tag value of its output. Then the behaviour of the generator can be described in terms of state transitions.

N:  After delivery of the last element of a run, change to state H. After delivery of the last element of the input stream, change to state F. Otherwise stay in state N. If the state is still N, advance to next item in input stream.

H:  Change state to N, advance to next item in input stream.

F:  Stay in state F.

The permissible state transitions are shown in Fig. 2.2. The node representing state N is doubly circled because the generator is to start in this state (unless the input stream is empty, in which case it is to start in state F).

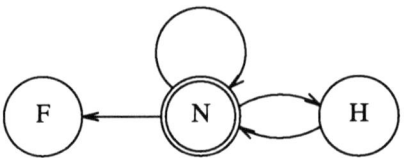

Fig. 2.2 -- State transitions of the run generator

Prog. 2.3 is a generator that satisfies the behaviour rules stated above. The generator should take its input from a file. However, to simplify the code, we have it reading data from an array *array*[1..*n*]. When the generator attains state F, it could continue to return the value *array*[*n*]. However, to allow for an empty input (the case *n*=0 here), we are requiring the user to supply a null value.

**generator** *runtagger*(*array*: integerarray; *n*: natural; *null*: valuetype):

<valuetype, tagtype>;

**persistent** *i*: natural; *value*: valuetype; *tag*: tagtype;

**begin**

if $n > 0$ then begin

value:= *array*[1]; *tag*:= N;

**suspend** <*value*, *tag*>;

*i*:= 2;

**while** $i \leq n$ **do begin**

**if** *array*[*i*] < *array*[*i*-1] **then**

**if** *tag* = H **then begin**

*value*:= *array*[*i*]; *tag*:= N;

*i*:= *i* + 1

>                   **end**
>               **else** *tag*:= H
>           **else begin**
>               *value*:= *array*[*i*];
>               *i*:= *i* + 1
>           **end**;
>           **suspend** <*value*, *tag*>
>       **end**
>   **end**;
>   **while** true **do**
>       **suspend** <*null*, F>
> **end** (* *runtagger* *)

Prog 2.3 -- A generator of runs

The very first action in merge sorting a sequence of values is to split the sequence into two streams of runs. Prog. 2.4 uses instance *runner* of generator *runtagger* to accomplish this.

switch := true;

cindex := 0;

dindex := 0;

runner(A, n, nullvalue) <value, tag>;

**while** tag ≠ F **do begin**

    **if** switch **then begin**

        cindex := cindex + 1;

        C[cindex] := value

    **end**

    **else begin**

        dindex := dindex + 1;

        D[dindex] := value

    **end**;

    runner(A, n, nullvalue) <value, tag>;

    **if** tag = H **then begin**

        switch := **not** switch;

        runner(A, n, nullvalue) <value, tag>

    **end**

**end**

Prog. 2.4 -- A program for the distribution of runs into two streams

In verifying Prog. 2.4 it must be shown that the generator attains state F (termination proof), and that the program does in fact distribute the runs. Termination can be demonstrated easily in an informal manner, as follows. If stream $A$ is empty, then the first call to *runner* puts it into state F, and the loop is not entered. When *runner* is not in state F, it advances to the next item in the input stream, except when it makes a transition from N to H (or from N to the termination state F). When *runner* is in state H, the next call lifts it out of this state, but at least one call to *runner* is made in every iteration of the loop.

The distribution is carried out properly if the following statements are true: (a) All elements of an input run go into the same output stream in the order that they have in the input run. (b) The input element that comes immediately after the elements of an input run does not go into the same output stream as the elements of this run. (c) Every element of the input goes into an output stream, and no element of the input goes twice into an output stream.

Let us show that the three statements are true. (a) When *switch* is true, all output is to $C$; otherwise it is to $D$. Now, by the nature of the generator, all elements of a run are delivered in sequence with their tags equal to N, and in Prog. 2.4 the value of *switch* is not changed while the tag is N. (b) But *switch* does change value when the tag is H. When the tag value is H, the generator delivers a datum that it has already delivered before, and the next element, delivered with tag N, goes into the output stream "opposite" to that used for the preceding run. (c) By the nature of the generator, the number of calls to *runner* is $n + k$, where $n$ is the number of elements in $A$, and $k$ is the number of runs they form. The latter cases correspond to tag values of H ($k$-1 times) and F (once). The former cases correspond to tag values of N, and it is easy to see that all $n$ such cases result in transfers to the output streams. Also, when the tag is H, *runner* is called again before a transfer to an output stream can be made, and there is no output when the tag is F. Consequently the number of transfers to the output streams is precisely $n$.

The tag values of *runtagger* make it easy to specify a program for two-way merge. This is done in Table 2.1. We assume that there is an initialization phase in which both generators are called, and that the input from the generators over $A$ and $B$ is in locations

*Aval* and *Bval*, respectively.

| AB | Action |
|---|---|
| NN | If *Aval* < *Bval* then output *Aval* and call generator over *A*, else output *Bval* and call generator over *B* |
| NH | Output *Aval* and call generator over *A* |
| NF | Output *Aval* and call generator over *A* |
| HN | Output *Bval* and call generator over *B* |
| HH | Call generator over *A* and *B*; switch output streams |
| HF | Call generator over *A*; switch output streams |
| FN | Output *Bval* and call generator over *B* |
| FH | Call generator over *B*; switch output streams |
| FF | HALT |

**Table 2.1** -- Tag-action table for two-way merge

The definition of generator *runtagger* and Table 2.1 constitute a full specification of two-way merge. The specification is abstract in the sense that it is independent of the nature of the input streams (files, linear arrays, instances of some other structure). Moreover, the specification easily generalizes to a three-way or a four-way merge. Only Table 2.1 needs to be changed (to one with 27 or 81 entries, respectively). Table 2.1 translates immediately into a program composed of nested case statements, part of which we show as Prog. 2.5. In Prog. 2.5 *Arunner* and *Brunner* are instances of a run generator for which the nature of its input data stream is left unspecified. Similarly, because the nature of the output data streams is also left open, procedure *transfer* is written in a schematic form.

The verification of Prog. 2.5 would be similar to that of Prog. 2.4: show that each generator attains state F, and that the program does in fact generate merged runs. However, it should not be difficult to convince oneself that Prog. 2.5 implements Table 2.1 faithfully. Therefore the verification can be developed in terms of Table 2.1. Informal demonstration of termination is quite easy. Consider the generator over $A$. Unless the generator is in state F, it advances to the next item in the input stream, except when it makes a transition from N to H (or from N to the termination state F). When the generator is in state H, the next call lifts it out of this state, and the only situation in which the next call is not forthcoming corresponds to the state combination HN. However, while this state combination persists, the generator over $B$ gets called, and ultimately the state of this generator has to become H.

The proof that merged runs are generated correctly should have three parts. (a) Given corresponding runs from $A$ and $B$, show that the output generated from these two runs is ordered, and that it all goes into the same output stream. (b) Show that after this output has been generated, output goes into the other output stream. (c) Show that after one input stream has become exhausted, the runs from the other input stream go alternately to one and the other output stream, and that a switchover of output streams takes place before the transfer of the first such run. The proof of these three parts would be similar to the proof of Prog. 2.4.

**var** *switch*: boolean; *Aval, Bval*: valuetype; *Atag, Btag*: tagtype;

**procedure** *transfer(value*: valuetype);

**begin**

    **if** *switch* **then** transfer *value* to stream *C*

    **else** transfer *value* to stream *D*

**end**; (* *transfer* *)

*switch*:= true;

*Arunner* <*Aval, Atag*>;

*Brunner* <*Bval, Btag*>;

**while** *Atag* ≠ F **or** *Btag* ≠ F **do begin**

    **case** *Atag* **of**

        N: **case** *Btag* **of**

            N: **if** *Aval* < *Bval* **then begin**

                *transfer(Aval)*;

                *Arunner* <*Aval, Atag*>

            **end**

            **else begin**

                *transfer(Bval)*;

                *Brunner* <*Bval, Btag*>

            **end**;

            H, F: **begin**

                *transfer(Aval)*;

                *Arunner* <*Aval, Atag*>

            **end**

        **end**;

        H: **case** *Btag* **of**

```
              ... ... ... ... ...
              ... ... ... ... ...

         F: case Btag of
              N: begin
                   transfer(Bval);
                   Brunner <Bval, Btag>
                 end;
              H: begin
                   Brunner <Bval, Btag>;
                   switch := not switch
                 end;
              F:  (* no operation *)
            end
          end
       end
```

Prog. 2.5 -- A two-way merge

The drawback of informal proofs is the difficulty to guarantee their completeness, that is, consideration of all possible cases. In the two-way merge problem all combinations of tag values are considered in Table 2.1, and we saw that the latter can be transformed into a program in a straightforward manner. Therefore, although a proof may be informal, it need not lack rigor. Even if no proof at all is undertaken, program reliability is improved by the requirement the method imposes that all tag-value combinations be examined in a disciplined manner.

## 2.4 UPDATING OF FILES

File update is our next example. One has a master file and a transaction file. The keys in the master file are unique, but the transaction file may contain a group of transaction records sharing the same key. The records within each group have to be sorted on the time of transaction. Since the sorting within a group could be made to produce at no additional cost a file in which the groups themselves are sorted on keys, we may as well stipulate that the transaction file is in fact so sorted. Transaction are of three types, I(nsertion), D(eletion), or C(hange), and the type is supplied as the value of a *transactiontype* field in a transaction record. The need for sorting the transaction file is illustrated by the following example. Suppose the transaction sequence in a group is CCDICC. Here the first two and the last two changes relate to different entities. Obviously the order of the changes is important. Note also that some transaction sequences are invalid, e.g., DCC and CCI. Valid transaction sequences correspond to paths in the transition diagram of Fig. 2.3.

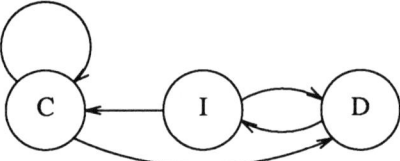

Fig. 2.3 -- Valid transaction sequences

As a general principle, the number of data types should be kept small, but here the master file and the transaction file must belong to different data types. First, there is the uniqueness of keys in one file but not the other. Second, the master file may be random, but the transaction file is not. Third, the transaction "file" need not be a single physical file. The transactions could arrive in separate streams from a number of sites. If both files were to be of the same type, then either the same operation would have to be implemented in different ways, or some operations would not be applicable to all objects of the one type. Neither situation is acceptable.

We propose two input generators, one for the old master, the other for the transaction file, and name their instances here *nextmaster* and *nexttransaction*, respectively. Both generators return records. The tag values returned by the master generator are L(ow), M(atch), H(igh), F(inished). The generator is supplied with a key, and values L, M, and H indicate how the key of the master record delivered by the generator relates to this key. If the last tag returned by *nextmaster* was H, then in the next call it returns the same record as before, but makes a new comparison of the key of this record to the key supplied to it, and the tag value may then change to L or M. If *nextmaster* is to get a record from a random file whose key matches the key of the transaction, then the only thing that matters is whether it finds or does not find such a record. If it finds the record, the tag value has to be M; otherwise it does not matter what it is (as long as it is not M). The transaction generator returns tag values N, O, F, which indicate that the transaction is the first of a group sharing the same key (N), or a subsequent transaction in the group (O), or that the iteration sequence has been exhausted (F). The transaction generator generates a sorted input stream (possibly from more than one transaction file). The generation of the input stream can well proceed in parallel with the actual update, but then we need a mechanism for waits in case the generator cannot produce the input stream at as fast a rate as it is consumed.

All generators we have seen so far have received their arguments just once, at the initial call to the generator. Here the tag that *nextmaster* associates with a record it delivers reflects the relationship between the key of this record and the key of the last record delivered by *nexttransaction*. The latter key has to be supplied to *nextmaster* as an argument (*recordT.key*) that may change from call to call. This argument is passed in the changing value mode discussed in Section 1.3.

*nexttransaction(streamT, nullrecord)* < *recordT, tagT*>;

**if** *tagT* ≠ F **then begin**

   **repeat**

      *nextmaster(fileM, recordT.key, nullrecord)* <*recordM, tagM*>;

      *sequentialtransfer1*;   (\* explained in the text \*)

      *recordpresent*:= (*tagM* = M);

      **if** *recordpresent* **then** *newrecord*:= *recordM*;

   **repeat**

      **if** *recordpresent* **then**

         **case** *recordT.transactiontype* **of**

            I:  ERROR CONDITION;

              C:  Make changes to *newrecord*;

            D:  **begin**

                  do deletion bookkeeping;

                  *recordpresent*:= false

              **end**

         **end**

      **else**

         **case** *recordT.transactiontype* **of**

            I:  **begin**

                  assemble in *newrecord* components of *recordT*;

                  *recordpresent*:= true

              **end**

            C, D:  ERROR CONDITION;

      **end**;

      *nexttransaction(streamT, nullrecord)* <*recordT, tagT*>

**until** *tagT*=N **or** *tagT*=F;

**if** *recordpresent* **then** *putrecord(newrecord)*

**until** *tagT* = F;

*sequentialtransfer2*;   (* explained in the text *)

**end**


Prog. 2.6 -- Updating of a master file


If the master file is sequential, then there are separate old and new masters, and records corresponding to keys for which there are no transactions still have to be transferred to the new master file. This is done in procedures *sequentialtransfer1* and *sequentialtransfer2* of Prog. 2.7. For a random master file, the bodies of *sequentialtransfer1* and *sequentialtransfer2* are empty.

Given a group of transaction records for the same key. If there exists a master record with this key, then the first transaction has to be of type C or D; if no master record exists, the first transaction has to be of type I. Prog. 2.6 checks that we start off correctly, and that only the transaction sequences indicated as valid by Fig. 2.3 are accepted.

Note that *putrecord* has only one argument. The file name is not given because the updated record of a random master file goes back into the same file, while in the sequential case there are separate old and new masters.

**procedure** *sequentialtransfer1*;

**begin**

    **while** *tagM* = L **do begin**

        *putrecord(recordM)*;

        *nextmaster(fileM, recordT.key, nullrecord)* <*recordM, tagM*>

    **end**

**end**;

**procedure** *sequentialtransfer2*;

**begin**

    **if** *tagM* = M **then**

        *nextmaster(fileM, recordT.key, nullrecord)* <*recordM, tagM*>;

    **while** *tagM* ≠ F **do begin**

        *putrecord(recordM)*;

        *nextmaster(fileM, recordT.key, nullrecord)* <*recordM, tagM*>

    **end**

**end**

Prog. 2.7 -- Record transfer procedures

Again the program verification proceeds by an analysis of all tag combinations, namely LN, LO, LF, MN, MO, MF, HN, HO, HF, FN, FO, FF. The combination FN did in fact point up an error in an earlier formulation of the file updating program. Let us discuss combinations LO, MF, and FN. Combination LO cannot arise. If *tagT* = O, then the process is in the repeat-until loop, in which there are no calls to *nextmaster*. But, before entry to the loop, *sequentialmaster1* made sure that *tagM* ≠ L. The combination MF arises when the transaction file has become exhausted, with *tagT* set to F by the *nexttransaction* in the last line of the repeat-until loop. If there is a *newrecord* to be put into the output, this will be done, and *sequentialtransfer2* is then called. It has to be watched that a record with the current *recordT.key* (which is equal to *recordM.key*) is not put into the output unnecessarily. Hence the test at the start of *sequentialtransfer2*. After that, all the unprocessed records from *fileM* are transferred into the output, again as expected. If there are no transactions to begin with, the entire process is bypassed. Combination FN arises when the master file has been exhausted, but there are still transactions to process. When the master file is empty to begin with, the first call to *nexttransaction* (line 1 of Prog. 2.6) is to result in $tagT = N$. Alternatively $tagT$ is to be set to N by the *nexttransaction* in the last line of the repeat-until loop. In either case, the call to *nextmaster* in line 3 of Prog. 2.6 returns the tag value F, the while loop in *sequentialtransfer1* is not entered, and *recordpresent* is set to false. This means that the only action is the assembling of a new record, as expected (unless the transaction type gives rise to an error condition).

The transaction generator can be used in the processing of any sequential sorted file with keys that are not unique. The generators could also be used to merge two sorted lists. We shall assume that each list consists of unique items, and that when an item appears in both lists, it is to be output just once. The problem is thus the finding of the union of two sets. Although comparison of keys in the merge procedure itself would more efficient than the use of tags, we shall develop the merge procedure from Prog. 2.6. This development can be seen as an instance of software reuse. We shall regard one of the lists to be merged as the "transaction file," and the other as the "master file." In the development of the initial version no attention at all will be paid to efficiency or elegance. Our only concern will be to cut out irrelevant parts from Prog. 2.6, and adapt the remaining parts to suit our requirements. The result is Prog. 2.8.

*nexttransaction(listA, nullitem) <itemA, tagA>;*

**while** *tagA ≠ F* **do begin**

    *nextmaster(listB, itemA, nullitem) <itemB, tagB>;*

    **while** *tagB = L* **do begin**

        *output(itemB);*

        *nextmaster(listB, itemA, nullitem) <itemB, tagB>*

    **end;**

    *match:= (tagB = M);*

    **if** *match* **then** *outitem:= itemB;*

    **repeat**

        **if not** *match* **then** *outitem:= itemA;*

        *nexttransaction(listA, nullitem) <itemA, tagA>;*

        *match:= true;*

    **until** *tagA=N* **or** *tagA=F;*

    **if** *match* **then** *output(outitem)*

**end;**

**if** *tagB = M* **then**

    *nextmaster(listB, itemA, nullitem) <itemB, tagB>;*

**while** *tagB ≠ F* **do begin**

    *output(itemB);*

    *nextmaster(listB, itemA, nullitem) <itemB, tagB>;*

**end**

Prog. 2.8 -- A merge program

The good feature about Prog. 2.8 is that it took about five minutes to change Progs. 2.6 and 2.7 into it, and that, if these programs are correct, then Prog. 2.8 is also likely to be correct. The bad feature is its appearance, but it took again only about five minutes to improve on it. For example, since in this application *tagT* always has the value N or F, the repeat-until loop of Prog. 2.8 is superfluous. Similar obvious improvements, based on reasoning about the program, gave rise to Prog. 2.9, and there is little to be gained in trying to improve this program still further.

>    *nexttransaction(listA, nullitem)* <*itemA, tagA*>;
>
> **while** *tagA* ≠ F **do begin**
>
>    *nextmaster(listB, itemA, nullitem)* <*itemB, tagB*>;
>
>    **while** *tagB* = L **do begin**
>
>       *output(itemB)*;
>
>       *nextmaster(listB, itemA, nullitem)* <*itemB, tagB*>
>
>    **end**;
>
>    *output(itemA)*;
>
>    *nexttransaction(listA, nullitem)* <*itemA, tagA*>;
>
> **end**;
>
> **if** *tagB* = M **then**
>
>    *nextmaster(listB, itemA, nullitem)* <*itemB, tagB*>;
>
> **while** *tagB* ≠ F **do begin**
>
>    *output(itemB)*;
>
>    *nextmaster(listB, itemA, nullitem)* <*itemB, tagB*>;
>
> **end**

Prog. 2.9 -- An improved merge program

## 2.5 A SPELLING CHECKER

A spelling checker extracts from an input text words that are not in its dictionary. The sorted list of these words is the output of the spelling checker. Some of the words may simply not have been included in the dictionary, and the user may add them to the dictionary. Others are spelling errors (or British spelling variants submitted to an American spelling checker). It helps to have a visual representation of the operations that are to produce the output, and data flow diagrams are often used for this purpose. Fig. 2.4 shows the structure of a spelling checker as a data flow diagram. The bubbles represent processes, arrows represent data flows, a rectangular box represents an external agent, and a pair of parallel lines represents a data store.

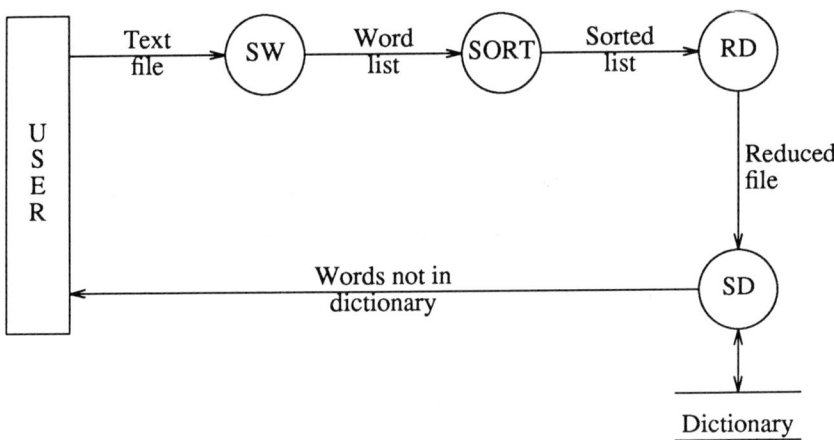

Fig. 2.4 -- Data flow diagram for a spelling checker

The spelling checker of Fig. 2.4 consists of four processes: SW transforms the input text into a sequence of words; SORT sorts the word; RD removes duplicates from the sorted list; and SD removes from the output RD the words that are found in the dictionary. Although the data flow diagram gives a clear indication of how the four processes are related, division of the task into these four processes is not necessarily the best way of dealing with the problem. This is a basic flaw in process-oriented design as such -- it tempts one into accepting a design that may not be the best for the problem under consideration. It is better to start with with a less detailed, that is, more abstract, specification because it allows greater implementation flexibility. The most abstract specification of the spelling checker merely states that it is to produce the set difference $T - D$, where $T$ stands for the set of words in the input text, and $D$ stands for the set of words in the dictionary. This set difference can be found in many ways. Let us look at a few possibilities.

A. The dictionary is a sorted list. The input, converted into a sorted list from which duplicates have been removed, is compared against the dictionary. The input conversion is achieved by --

    a. the sequence of actions shown in Fig. 2.4;

    b. construction of a heap, and extraction of elements in sorted order from the heap, with duplicates removed at this extraction stage;

    c. input words put into an AVL tree if they are not already in this tree, and the tree used to produce a sorted output.

B. The dictionary is a hash table. Each input word is searched for in the dictionary, and words that are not found are --

    a. put into an AVL tree if they are not already in this tree, and the tree is later used to produce a sorted output; or

    b. put into a list that is subsequently sorted and duplicates removed.

The selection of the best solution from these five alternatives will be determined by to word type counts in the input. Each of the alternatives provides an opportunity for the use of generators. For example, the input sequence of words can be produced by a generator. Under alternative Aa, process SORT can be implemented as heapsort consisting of a procedure and a generator, as discussed in Section 1.3. Duplicate removal could then be overlapped with the generation of the sorted output by process SORT, and, regarding RD as another generator, with the dictionary comparisons.

Let us consider alternative Ac in detail. Here we have two major phases: the construction of the AVL tree and the dictionary comparisons. In the first phase the AVL tree constructor calls the input word generator, and either finds that the word supplied by the generator is already in the tree or that this word has to be inserted in the AVL tree. This phase is completed when the entire input has been processed. The second phase is based on the dictionary comparison process, which may be implemented as a procedure that builds up the set difference $T - D$. This process calls a generator that traverses the AVL tree under inorder and returns the next word that is to be compared against the dictionary. The dictionary words, too, can be supplied by a generator. The program that carries out the comparison process was developed from Prog. 2.6, rather than from Prog. 2.9 because Prog. 2.6 is more general. Again an initial rough version of the comparison program was created first, and this refined into Prog. 2.10, at a total cost of at most 10 minutes.

Instance *nextdictword* belongs to the same generator as *nextmaster*. This means that when *nextdictword* is called while *tagD* = H from its previous call, it keeps returning the same value. A spelling checker is a program that is likely to be produced in many copies, and to be extensively used. This is therefore an instance of an inefficiency that should be eliminated by specialization of the generator.

>     *nexttextword(AVL, nullword) <textword, tagT>;*
>
> **while** *tagT* ≠ F **do begin**
>
> > *nextdictword(dict, textword, nullword) <dictword, tagD>;*
> >
> > **while** *tagD* = L **do**
> >
> > > *nextdictword(dict, textword, nullword) <dictword, tagD>;*
> >
> > **if** *tagD* ≠ M **then** *output(textword);*
> >
> > *nexttextword(AVL, nullword) <textword, tagT>*
>
> **end**

      Prog 2.10 -- Listing of text words not in the dictionary

## 2.6 THE PROBLEM OF DOUBLED CHARACTERS

This is again a toy example, but it is interesting because an extensive discussion on the merits of coroutines in the late 1970s centered around it. There are two processes. Process A copies characters from an input, but every "aa" in the input is converted to a "b"; process B copies characters from the output of A to its own output, but converts every "bb" to a "c". Again the English specification is imprecise. We presume that both "aab" and "baa" are to end up as "c", but what is to happen with "bbb"? Is the result to be "cb" or "bc"? We shall assume that in a case such as this the leftmost two characters are converted.

Our version of the program, shown as Prog. 2.11, is the generator *doubles* that embeds another generator. The embedded generator is called *inner*, and *inner* also denotes the instance of it that is used by *doubles*. The input to the entire process is supplied by yet another generator, whose instance *input* is called by the embedded generator. An instance of *doubles*, to which we give the name *fixer*, will be called as follows:

*fixer*("a", "b", "c", "#") <*char, tag*>

Let us use the names of the generators rather than of their instances in what follows. A call to *doubles* causes it to make a single call or two calls to *inner,* depending on what happened when *inner* was called the last time. If there was then an output of a "c" caused by *inner* finding two "b"s in its input, then *inner* is called twice. If this time there is no duplication, then the first character is delivered to *doubles,* and the second character is saved for reference. The call that *inner* makes to *input* has a similar effect there.

**generator** *doubles(first, middle, last, nullch*: character): <character, tagtype>;

**generator** *inner(inch, ouch, nullch*: character): <character, tagtype>;

**gen** *input*: *charactergenerator*;

**persistent** *ch1*: character; *tag1*: tagtype;

**temporary** *ch2*: character; *tag2*: tagtype;

**begin**

*input(nullch)* <*ch1, tag1*>;

**while** true **do begin**

*input(nullch)* <*ch2, tag2*>;

**if** *tag2* = F **then begin**

**if** *tag1* ≠ F **then suspend** <*ch1*, N>;

**while** true **do suspend** <*nullch*, F>

**end**;

**if** *ch1=ch2* **and** *ch1=inch* **then begin**

**suspend** <*ouch*, N>; *input(nullch)* <*ch1, tag1*>

**end**

**else begin**

**suspend** <*ch1*, N>; *ch1*:= *ch2*

                end
            end
        end
    **gen** *inner*: *inner*;
    **persistent** *ch1*: character; *tag1*: tagtype;
    **temporary** *ch2*: character; *tag2*: tagtype;
**begin**
    *inner(initial, middle, nullch)* <*ch1, tag1*>;
    **while** true **do begin**
        *inner(initial, middle, nullch)* <*ch2, tag2*>;
        **if** *tag2* = F **then begin**
            **if** *tag1* ≠ F **then suspend** <*ch1*, N>;
            **while** true **do suspend** <*nullch*, F>
        **end**;
        **if** *ch1=ch2* **and** *ch1=middle* **then begin**
            **suspend** <*last*, N>; *inner(initial, middle, nullch)* <*ch1, tag1*>;
        **end**
        **else begin**
            **suspend** <*ch1*, N>; *ch1*:= *ch2*
        **end**
    **end**
**end** (* *doubles* *)

Prog. 2.11 -- A text transformer

Generators *doubles* and *inner* have a very similar structure. If a programming language provides the appropriate features, it would be feasible to have them as two instances of the same generator. Here, however, we shall not go into programming language design. Moreover, the reasons for wanting to have only one generator should be examined. One is that less permanent storage space is needed. Today such concerns for minor storage economy have become largely irrelevant, except with embedded software, say in a refrigerator. In the latter case, even if one were to save no more than a few pounds or dollars by having a smaller storage unit, the total becomes significant when the number of refrigerators is 100,000 or so. Another reason is standardization. A generator should be written in such a way that it can be used in multiple applications, should the opportunity arise, but it is unlikely that there will be much demand for the character replacement operation discussed here.

## 2.7 MULTIPLICATION OF MATRICES

Although matrix multiplication appears to be a straightforward operation, the efficiency of the operation is determined to a very large degree by the architecture of the computer on which the operation is carried out. It depends also on the programming language. For example, Fortran stores the elements of a matrix in column order. The alternative is row-order storage. For elements of a $2 \times 2$ matrix $A$, row order is

$$a_{11} \quad a_{12} \quad a_{21} \quad a_{22}$$

while column order is

$$a_{11} \quad a_{21} \quad a_{12} \quad a_{22}$$

Under some machine architectures, access to sequentially stored data is faster than access to the same data when they are not stored sequentially. One should therefore avoid operations on two matrices that require one matrix to be accessed in row order and the other in column order. In particular, Fortran programs should access all matrices in column order.

Let us consider matrices $A$ and $B$, which we regard as functions:

$$A: 1..n \times 1..t \rightarrow Numtype;$$
$$B: 1..t \times 1..m \rightarrow Numtype.$$

Then their product, the matrix $C$, is another function,

$$C: 1..n \times 1..m \rightarrow Numtype,$$

such that

$$\forall\ i: i \in 1..n: (\forall\ j: j \in 1..m: (C(i,j) = \sum_{k=1}^{k=t}(A(i,k) \times B(k,j)))).$$

The implementation code will contain the statement

$$C(i,j) := C(i,j) + A(i,k) * B(k,j)$$

and the statement will be inside three nested loops. The order of the loop statements makes much difference. The ordering

> **for** $i := 1, n$ **do**
> **for** $j := 1, m$ **do**
> **for** $k := 1, t$ **do**

is the conventional approach in which the elements of $C$ are built up one at a time. Under ordering

> **for** $i := 1, n$ **do**
> **for** $k := 1, t$ **do**
> **for** $j := 1, m$ **do**

the elements of $C$ are built up one row at a time, but under

**for** $k:= 1, t$ **do**

**for** $i:= 1, n$ **do**

**for** $j:= 1, m$ **do**

every element of $C$ is added to in each of the $t$ iterations of the outer loop.

In Section 1.1 we already alluded to matrix multiplication as the processing of data streams. Here we shall explore this approach in some detail. During the matrix multiplication process various elements of the matrices $A$ and $B$ are being accessed. If we write down the order in which they are accessed, we get a list of elements. This list of elements can be regarded as defining a data stream. To keep the examples simple, we shall consider $2 \times 2$ matrices. The two streams of Section 1.1, namely

$$a_{11} \quad a_{12} \quad a_{21} \quad a_{22} \quad a_{11} \quad a_{12} \quad a_{21} \quad a_{22}$$

which consists of a sequence of all the elements of $A$ in row order delivered twice, and

$$b_{11} \quad b_{21} \quad b_{11} \quad b_{21} \quad b_{12} \quad b_{22} \quad b_{12} \quad b_{22}$$

which delivers each column of $B$ twice before starting on the next column, produce the output, one element at a time, in column order,

$$c_{11} \quad c_{21} \quad c_{12} \quad c_{22}$$

To get the output in row order, which is

$$c_{11} \quad c_{12} \quad c_{21} \quad c_{22}$$

the input streams have to be

$$a_{11} \quad a_{12} \quad a_{11} \quad a_{12} \quad a_{21} \quad a_{22} \quad a_{21} \quad a_{22}$$
$$b_{11} \quad b_{21} \quad b_{12} \quad b_{22} \quad b_{11} \quad b_{21} \quad b_{12} \quad b_{22}$$

so, irrespective of whether the output is produced in column order or row order, one of the inputs has to follow row order, the other column order.

When an entire row of the output is generated at the same time, we need three input streams: elements of A, elements of B, and the partially built-up elements of C, but now there is greater uniformity in that all the streams are in row order --

$$\begin{array}{cccccccc} a_{11} & & a_{12} & & a_{21} & & a_{22} & \\ b_{11} & b_{12} & b_{21} & b_{22} & b_{11} & b_{12} & b_{21} & b_{22} \\ c_{11} & c_{12} & c_{11} & c_{12} & c_{21} & c_{22} & c_{21} & c_{22} \end{array}$$

Here the matrix A is delivered once, but B is delivered as many times as there are rows in A. All the matrices are accessed in row order; for access in column order the ordering of the loop statements should be

**for** $j := 1, n$ **do**

**for** $k := 1, t$ **do**

**for** $i := 1, m$ **do**

Our discussion has shown that one can improve on the conventional way of coding a matrix multiplication program. The third variant, in which each iteration over $k$ contributes to every element of C, does not have to be discussed in detail because it inherits the bad features of the other variants. In this variant elements from A follow column order, elements from B follow row order, and we still need the third stream of partially computed elements of C.

The streams we discussed above could be produced by generators. There is no point in using generators for ordinary matrices, but when the matrices are sparse, that is, the number of their nonzero elements is only a small fraction of their total number of elements, then generators can be useful. The sparseness of a matrix or the lack of it is measured by its density, which is the ratio of its nonzero elements to its total number of elements. Given matrices A and B, with densities $d_a$ and $d_b$, respectively, such that the number of columns in A (and the number of rows in B) is $k$, it can be shown that under some not very stringent assumptions the density of the matrix product $AB$ is given by $1 - (1 - d_a d_b)^k$. From this expression we find that the density of the product of two $80 \times 80$ matrices, both with densities 0.10, is 0.55. In general, then, the product of two sparse matrices cannot be expected to be sparse. Hence, in the example that follows, we shall store the product of two sparse matrices as a conventional two-dimensional array.

Let us take the approach in which the product matrix is built up one entire row at a time. The same generator can then be used to supply elements of both $A$ and $B$. A sparse matrix is commonly represented by a set of triples, one for each nonzero element, consisting of the row index, the column index, and the value of the element, with the triples ordered on the indices. However, our generator is to operate on a representation that for the matrix

$$FourBySix = \begin{bmatrix} 3 & 8 & 0 & 0 & 0 & 2 \\ 0 & 0 & 0 & 0 & 0 & 0 \\ 7 & 0 & 2 & 0 & 0 & 3 \\ 2 & 1 & 0 & 7 & 0 & 0 \end{bmatrix}$$

consists of a row entry vector

$$R = [\ 1\ \ 4\ \ 4\ \ 7\ \ 10\ ]$$

and a two-row matrix

$$M = \begin{bmatrix} 1 & 2 & 6 & 1 & 3 & 6 & 1 & 2 & 4 \\ 3 & 8 & 2 & 7 & 2 & 3 & 2 & 1 & 7 \end{bmatrix}.$$

The second row of $M$ holds the value of an element, and the first row the number of the column in which it is found in *FourBySix*. The row number of the element can be obtained from $R$. For a matrix of $k$ rows, $R$ has $k+1$ elements, $R(j+1)-R(j)$ indicates the number of nonzero elements in row $j$ of *FourBySix*, and, if this number is greater than zero, $R(j)$ gives the number of the column in $M$ in which storage of the nonzero elements of row $j$ of *FourBySix* starts.

Let us look again at the order in which elements of 2 × 2 matrices $A$ and $B$ have to be accessed for our multiplication scheme:

$$a_{11} \quad\quad a_{12} \quad\quad a_{21} \quad\quad a_{22}$$
$$b_{11} \quad b_{12} \quad b_{21} \quad b_{22} \quad b_{11} \quad b_{12} \quad b_{21} \quad b_{22}$$

If $a_{ij} = 0$, then, of course, all $a_{ij} \times b_{j1}$, $a_{ij} \times b_{j2}$, ..... are zero as well, that is, the row of $B$ that corresponds to the $a_{ij}$, namely $[b_{j1}, b_{j2}, .....]$, does not have to be generated. Therefore we want our generator for $A$ to deliver all its nonzero elements, but the generator for $B$ to skip the rows that are not needed. Further, because $B$ has to be traversed as many times as there are nonzero rows in $A$, the generator should start delivering the elements of its input matrix all over again after it has finished one traversal of the matrix. Suppose *FourBySix* is our $A$. Then we would want the generator to deliver the rows of $B$ (or, rather, the nonzero elements in these rows) in the order 1, 2, 6, 1, 3, 6, 1, 2, 4.

We shall have a changing input argument *nextrow*. When this is zero, the generator will deliver the elements of the sparse matrix in normal row order. However, when *nextrow = k* ($k > 0$), the generator will skip to row $k$. Care then has to be taken in the design of the multiplication program, because, if $k$ is not reset to zero, the generator will keep on delivering the first nonzero element of row $k$. Another problem that can arise is that the row to which the generator is asked to skip has no nonzero elements. This we solve with tags. We have three tags: N(ormal), associated with a nonzero element in a row; E(nd), returned after the end of a row of the matrix has been reached; F(inish), returned after the end of the matrix has been reached. When the matrix has a row with all zero elements, then the generator returns tag E on entry to this row, and the next call to the generator will be an advance to the next row. When the last row of the matrix has all zero elements, then the generator returns first E, and then F. After the call that returns tag F, a new traversal of the matrix starts. When the tag value is E or F, the element value returned by the generator is the null value supplied by the caller of the generator, but the returned row and column numbers are meaningless. Just as with generator *runtagger* (Prog. 2.3), in the interests of simpler coding we are willing to accept the inefficiency of having calls that do not return data.

Prog. 2.12 is a generator of the elements of a sparse matrix represented by arrays *R* and *M*. If the entire representation is named *mat*, then the qualified references *mat.R* and *mat.M* give access to its two components. We assume the availability of function *size*, which returns the number of elements of an array. Thus, $size(FourBySix) = 24$, $size(mat.R) = 5$.

**generator** *roworder*(*matrix*: sparseform; *null*: valuetype; **changing** *nextrow*: natural):

&lt;valuetype, natural, natural, tagtype&gt;;

**persistent** *i, row*: natural;

**temporary** *value*: valuetype; *col*: natural; *tag*: tagtype;

**begin**

    *i*:= 0; *row*:= 1;

    **while** true **do begin**

        **if** *nextrow* ≠ 0 **then begin**

            *row*:= *nextrow*;

            *i*:= *matrix.R*[*row*];

        **end**

        **else** *i*:= *i* + 1;

        **if** *i* = *matrix.R*[*row*+1] **then begin**

            *value*:= *null*; *row*:= 1; *col*:= 0;

            *tag*:= E

        **end**

        **else if** *row* = *size*(*matrix.R*) **then begin**

            *value*:= *null*; *row*:= 1; *col*:= 0;

>    *tag* := F;
>
>    *i* := 0
>
>  **end**
>
>  **else begin**
>
>    *value* := *matrix.M*[*i*, 2];
>
>    *col* := *matrix.M*[*i*, 1];
>
>    *tag* := N
>
>  **end**
>
>  **suspend** <*value, row, col, tag*>
>
> **end**
>
> **end** (* *roworder* *)

Prog. 2.12 -- Generator of elements of a sparse matrix

The substance of the generator consists of two if statements. The first selects the column of *M* that is to be looked at. If *nextrow* ≠ 0, then, instead of a normal traversal of the array, a jump is made to the row indicated by *nextrow*. The second if statement differentiates between a call made after the last element of a row has been delivered, a call made after the last element of the entire matrix has been delivered, and a call made after an element other than the last element of a row has been delivered. When an instance of *roworder* is applied to our representation of *FourBySix*, the first fifteen calls with *nextrow* = 0 will return <3, 1, 1, N>, <8, 1, 2, N>, <2, 1, 6, N>, <null, 1, 0, E>, <null, 1, 0, E>, <7, 3, 1, N>, <2, 3, 3, N>, <3, 3, 6, N>, <null, 1, 0, E>, <2, 4, 1, N>, <1, 4, 2, N>, <7, 4, 4, N>, <null, 1, 0, F>, <3, 1, 1, N>, <8, 1, 2, N>.

The matrix multiplication program in terms of the generator of Prog. 2.12 is Prog. 2.13, where *matrixA* and *matrixB* are instances of *roworder*, and *repA* and *repB* are representations of sparse matrices $A$ and $B$.

>**for** $i := 1$ **to** $n$ **do**
>**for** $j := 1$ **to** $m$ **do**
>>$C[i, j] := 0.0$;
>
>**repeat**
>>$matrixA(repA, null, 0)$ <$valA, rowA, colA, tagA$>
>
>**until** $tagA = N$ **or** $tagA = F$;
>**while** $tagA \neq F$ **do begin**
>>$matrixB(repB, null, colA)$ <$valB, rowB, colB, tagB$>;
>>**while** $tagB = N$ **do begin**
>>>$C[rowA, colB] := C[rowA, colB] + valA * valB$;
>>>$matrixB(repB, null, 0)$ <$valB, rowB, colB, tagB$>
>>
>>**end**;
>>**repeat**
>>>$matrixA(repA, null, 0)$ <$valA, rowA, colA, tagA$>
>>
>>**until** $tagA = N$ **or** $tagA = F$
>
>**end**

Prog. 2.13 -- Multiplication of two sparse matrices

After matrix $C$ is initialized to a null matrix, a search is made for the first nonzero element of $A$. If there is no such element ($A$ is a null matrix), then an exit is made from the repeat-until with $tagA = F$, and the while loop that follows is not entered -- that is, $C$ remains a null matrix. Otherwise the nonzero element is multiplied with nonzero elements of the corresponding row of $B$. After this, the next nonzero element is searched for, it is multiplied with the nonzero elements of the corresponding row of $B$, and so forth, until all elements of $A$ have been processed.

# 3

# The Generate-and-Test Paradigm

When a problem does not admit a customized algorithmic solution, one has to resort to backtracking. Backtracking is an instance of the generate-and-test approach. Under generate-and-test, potential solutions or partial solutions to a problem are generated, and their effectiveness is then tested. As far as practicable, the generation and test phases are implemented as separate modules. This means that when the criterion that the solution has to satisfy is changed, only the test module needs to be changed. Alternatively, changes in the strategy for the generation of potential partial solutions do not affect the test component. We also discuss generators in Reggia's model of diagnostic inference.

## 3.1 THE QUEENS PROBLEM

Chess is played on a board with 64 squares arranged in 8 rows of 8 squares each. An important chess piece is the queen because it can capture an opponent's piece that lies in the same row as the queen, in the same column as the queen, or on the same two diagonals as the queen. Fig. 3.1 shows the capture potential of a queen located in row 4 and column 3 of the board. Note that we count rows from the top of the board, and columns from its left.

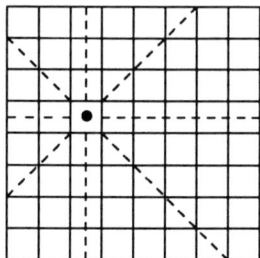

Fig. 3.1 -- The capture potential of a queen

The 8-queens problem requires eight queens to be placed on an 8 × 8 board so that they cannot capture each other. Fig. 3.2 shows one solution of the problem (of a total of 92).

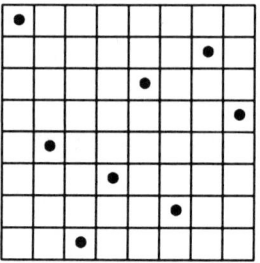

Fig. 3.2 -- A solution of the 8-queens problem

In a more general form the problem is defined for an $n \times n$ board, and it becomes the $n$-queens problem. The solution for $n = 1$ is to put a queen in the single square of the board. There are no solutions for $n = 2$ and $n = 3$, two solutions for $n = 4$, and ten for $n = 5$. Fig. 3.3 shows the two solutions for $n = 4$. These two solutions illustrate the general phenomenon that the number of "independent" solutions is smaller than the total number of solutions. A set of independent solutions is a minimal set from which all other solutions can be obtained by symmetry transformations. Here, for example, the second solution is obtained from the first by flipping the board around the horizontal or the vertical axis, or either of the diagonal axes, or by rotating the board in the plane through $180^0$. The 8-queens problem has 12 independent solutions.

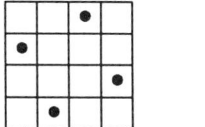
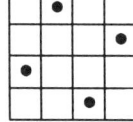

Fig. 3.3 -- Solutions of the 4-queens problem

If one's livelihood depended on finding solutions to the *n*-queens problem most efficiently, the symmetries could be exploited. For us the problem has different significance. Instead of being concerned with efficiency that derives from special properties of the problem, we shall use the problem to introduce the generate-and-test paradigm, which is a general approach to the development of some kinds of software. Let us first formulate the *n*-queens problem as the construction of a Boolean function $Q$,

$$Q: 1..n \times 1..n \longrightarrow Boolean,$$

which is to be true for a square <*i, j*> if it contains a queen, and false otherwise. The solution shown in the left diagram of Fig. 3.3 is then defined by $Q(1, 3) = Q(2, 1) = Q(3, 4) = Q(4, 2) =$ true, and $Q$ false for all other arguments. In general, function $Q$ is a solution of the *n*-queens problem if predicate *NQueens(n)* holds:

*NQueens* $(n) =$
  $\forall\ i:\ 1 \leq i \leq n:$
    $\exists\ j:\ 1 \leq j \leq n:\ (Q(i, j)$
      $\wedge\ \forall\ s:\ 1 \leq s \leq i-1 \vee i+1 \leq s \leq n:\ (\text{not } Q(s, j))$
      $\wedge\ \forall\ t:\ 1 \leq t \leq j-1 \vee j+1 \leq t \leq n:\ (\text{not } Q(i, t))$

$$\wedge \ \forall \ s: \ 1 \leq s \leq i-1 \vee i+1 \leq s \leq n: \ ($$
$$\forall \ t: \ 1 \leq t \leq j-1 \vee j+1 \leq t \leq n: \ ($$
$$s+t = i+j \ \rightarrow \ \text{not } Q(s,t) \wedge$$
$$s-t = i-j \ \rightarrow \ \text{not } Q(s,t))))).$$

The definition of *NQueens* consists of four conjuncts. The first states that there is a queen in each row (for each row there exists a column in which a queen is located). Fixing the position of this queen at <$i, j$>, the other three conjuncts indicate that there is no other queen in row $i$, in column $j$, or on the southwest-northeast and southeast-northwest diagonals through <$i, j$>.

Under the generate-and-test approach, a candidate solution $Q$ is generated, and this $Q$ is tested by evaluating the *NQueens* predicate for it. The generation of all functions $Q$ is out of the question. For example, the number of functions from $1..8 \times 1..8$ to {true, false} is $2^{64}$, which, expressed as a decimal integer, has 20 digits. We can reduce this number considerably by noting that there is to be precisely one queen in each column. This suggests the compact representation of $Q$ by an 8-element vector $S$ shown in Fig. 3.4, where $S[j] = i$ means that $Q(i, j)$ is true.

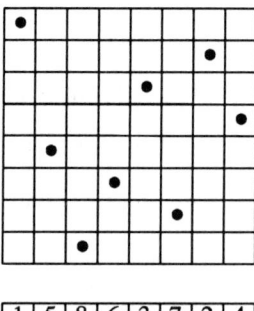

Fig. 3.4 -- A representation for the 8-queens problem

The total number of possibilities has been reduced to $8^8 = 2^{24} = 16,772,216$. This is still high, but we can reduce the number further by generating partial solutions. For example, neither the configuration

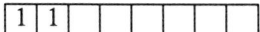

nor the configuration

can lead to a solution, that is, there can be no solution for which $S[1] = S[2] = 1$, or for which $S[1] = 1$ and $S[2] = 2$. This alone excludes $2 \times 8^6 = 524,288$ of the 16,772,216 possibilities.

The generation and testing components of the solution process have to be interrelated to allow suppression of the generation of configurations that cannot lead to a solution, but they should be separate activities. Suppose that the first $k - 1$ entries of the $n$-element solution vector represent queens that cannot capture each other, and that the generator now sets $S[k] = i$ (which corresponds to $Q(i, j)$ being true). The test component checks that the $k$th queen represented by this entry in $S$ is safe from capture by the previously placed $k - 1$ queens, by evaluating the following adaptation of *NQueens*:

$$\forall\ t\colon\ 1 \le t \le k-1\colon\ (\text{not}\ Q(i,t))$$
$$\wedge\ \forall\ s\colon\ 1 \le s \le i-1 \vee i+1 \le s \le n\colon\ ($$
$$s+t = i+k\ \longrightarrow\ \text{not}\ Q(s,t)\ \wedge$$
$$s-t = i-k\ \longrightarrow\ \text{not}\ Q(s,t))), \tag{3.1}$$

which, in terms of representation $S$, is implemented as Prog. 3.1. The $i$ and $k$ of expression (3.1) are fixed ordinal numbers, and $s$ also has to be an ordinal number. This means that for a particular $t$ there is at most one $s$ that satisfies $s+t = i+k$, and at most one $s$ that satisfies $s-t = i-k$, and we rewrite (3.1) as

$$\forall\, t:\ 1 \le t \le k-1:\ (\text{not } Q(i,t)\ \wedge$$
$$\text{not } Q(t-i-k,t)\ \wedge$$
$$\text{not } Q(t+i-k,t)). \tag{3.2}$$

Although expression (3.2) does not exclude $t - i - k \le 0$ and $t + i - k \le 0$, for which $Q$ is outside its domain of definition, this does not matter because the problem disappears when (3.2) is reformulated in terms of $S$. Given that $S[k] = i$, we require that $S[t] \neq i$, $S[t] \neq t - i - k$, and $S[t] \neq t + i - k$, and, writing $S[k]$ for $i$, we obtain the formulation of Prog. 3.1.

**function** *testsolution*(*S*: array[1..*n*], *k*: ordinal): boolean;

    **var** *t*: ordinal; *ok*: boolean;

**begin**

    *ok*:= true;

    **for** *t*:= 1 **to** *k*-1 **do begin**

        *ok*:= *ok* **and not** $S[k] = S[t]$;

        *ok*:= *ok* **and not** $S[k]+k = S[t]+t$;

        *ok*:= *ok* **and not** $S[k]-k = S[t]-t$;

    **end**;

    *testsolution*:= *ok*

**end** (* *testsolution* *)

Prog. 3.1 -- Test routine for the *n*-queens problem

If Prog. 3.1 returns true for $S[k] = i$, then the generator will try to extend $S$ by setting $S[k+1] = 1$. Otherwise it will generate a configuration in which $S[k] = i+1$. However, if Prog. 3.1 returns false, and $S[k] = n$, then backtracking has to be undertaken. Here this means that $S[k-1]$, $S[k-2]$, ..., $S[1]$ are examined in turn, and as soon as a $j$ is found such that $S[j] < n$, the new partial solution to be tested is $S^*[1] = S[1]$, ..., $S^*[j-1] = S[j-1]$, $S^*[j] = S[j]+1$. If no such $j$ is found, then the process stops.

Keeping generation and testing separate improves program clarity. Another advantage is that when the test component is independent of the generator algorithm, changes in the latter need not affect the former. The generator for the $n$-queens problem is shown as Prog. 3.3. Prog. 3.2, which finds all solutions of the 8-queens problem, is written in terms of instance *placequeen* of Prog. 3.3.

>*ok*:= true;
>
>**repeat**
>
>>*placequeen*(8, *ok*) <*solution, k*>;
>>
>>**if** $k > 0$ **then** *ok*:= *testsolution*(*solution, k*);
>>
>>**if** *ok* **and** $k=8$ **then begin**
>>
>>>*output*(*solution*, 8);
>>>
>>>*ok*:= false
>>
>>**end**
>
>**until** $k=0$

Prog. 3.2 -- Program for all solutions of the 8-queens problem

**generator** *nextconfiguration*(*n*: ordinal; **changing** *ok*: boolean): <array[1..*n*], integer>;

   **persistent** *k*: integer; *solution*: array[1..*n*];

   **temporary** *i*: integer; *trynext*: boolean;

**begin**

   *k*:= 0;

   **while true do begin**

```
    if ok and k<n then begin
        k:= k + 1;
        solution[k]:= 1
    end
    else begin
        trynext:= true;
        while trynext and k ≥ 1 do
            if solution[k] < n then begin
                solution[k]:= solution[k] + 1;
                trynext:= false
            end
            else k:= k - 1
        end;
        if k ≥ 1 then suspend <solution, k>
        else begin
            for i:= 1 to n do solution[i]:= 0;
            while true do suspend <solution, 0>
        end
    end
end (* placequeen *)
```

Prog. 3.3 -- Configuration generator for the *n*-queens problem

## 3.2 BACKTRACKING

Consider the 3-queens problem. Here the generator of Prog. 3.3 would deliver configurations [1**], [11*], [12*], [13*], [131], [132], [133], [2**], [21*], [22*], [23*], [3**], [31*], [311], [312], [313], [32*], and [33*]. The process of generation of the configurations is illustrated by the tree of Fig. 3.5, where the configurations as listed above are obtained by carrying out a preorder traversal of the tree, and reading off the node labels on the path from the root to the node currently reached. A cross through a node indicates that Prog. 3.1 has returned false for the corresponding configuration. Since every terminal node in the tree is crossed out, the 3-queens problem has no solution.

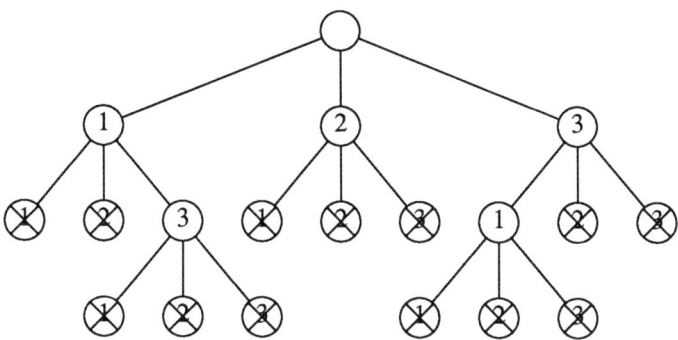

Fig. 3.5 -- Configurations for the 3-queens problem

The configurations do not necessarily have to be generated in the order defined by preorder traversal of the the tree of Fig. 3.5. Prog. 3.1 would still be the appropriate test routine for configuration [*abcd*...] as long as Prog. 3.1 had already returned true for configuration [*abc*...]. In terms of the tree, the configuration corresponding to any node in the tree may be generated as long as the configuration represented by its parent has already been generated. Under this approach to the $n$-queens problem as discussed in Section 3.1, a change in the order that configurations are generated makes little difference, but there are other problems for which there is a significant difference in the effort needed to find a solution. Also, there is no reason why a solution of the $n$-queens problem should be built up in the order of the columns from left to right. However, a change in this order would require a change to function *testsolution* as well.

Let us now collect the observations we have been making into a proper definition of backtracking. Given a Cartesian product of a finite number of finite domains

$$A = A_1 \times A_2 \times \cdots \times A_k, \tag{3.3}$$

consider all $k$-tuples from $A$ as candidates for the solution of a problem, where a candidate is acceptable as a solution if it satisfies some given criterion. Cases in which the solution may vary in length, that is, the number of elements defining a solution may be less than $k$, can be provided for by including special null elements in the $A_i$.

A solution is generated by means of extension steps, in which a partial solution $<a_1, a_2, ..., a_i>$, $i<k$, is extended to $<a_1, a_2, ..., a_i, a_{i+1}>$, and so forth, until a $k$-tuple $<a_1, a_2, ..., a_k>$ is obtained that hopefully satisfies the solution criterion. However, if it is established from examination of the partial solution $<a_1, a_2, ..., a_i>$ that no extension of this partial solution can lead to a solution, then a backtracking step is taken. This means tracking back to the partial solution $<a_1, a_2, ..., a_{i-1}>$ and extending it by an as yet untried value from $A_i$.

The Cartesian product (3.3) can be represented by a tree in which each $<a_1, a_2, ..., a_k> \in A$ is represented by the path (root, $a_1, a_2, ..., a_k$) All candidate solutions that derive from the one partial solution $<a_1, a_2, ..., a_i>$, $i<k$, share the same subpath (root, $a_1, a_2, ..., a_i$), and the number of terminal nodes in the tree is equal to the

number of $k$-tuples in $A$. On finding that $<a_1, a_2, ..., a_i>$ cannot be extended, one backs up in the tree to node $a_{i-1}$ (hence "backtrack"), "blocks" the arc from node $a_{i-1}$ to node $a_i$, thus preventing access to the subtree rooted at node $a_i$, and moves down from $a_{i-1}$ to a node as yet unvisited. If no such unvisited node remains, one backs up to $a_{i-2}$, and so forth.

The interpretation of backtracking can be liberalized by accepting any traversal of the tree in which blocking takes place as described above, and both after a blocking operation or as an extension step any as yet unvisited node may be visited next, subject only to the requirement that no node may be visited before its parent has been visited. Under this interpretation a pool of partial solutions is maintained, and any solution in the pool may be selected for extension. Moreover, the traversal strategy need not be predefined, that is, it may evolve during the traversal.

Sometimes an *ab initio* restriction may limit solutions to a subset of $A$. Although this case can be covered by making the restriction part of the solution criterion, greater efficiency can be obtained by building the restriction into the generator of partial solutions. The tree would then be appropriately reduced, and the definition of the backtracking process adapted accordingly.

## 3.3 A SHORTEST PATH PROBLEM

Given a rooted tree that contains a finite set of nodes. For each node, *arclength* indicates the length of the arc that terminates at this node -- for the root of the tree we have *arclength* = 0. It is required to find the length of the shortest of the paths from the root to terminal nodes. The basis of the algorithm is to maintain in *best* the length of the path that is shortest in terms of the paths already examined; *best* is initialized to a very large number. The strategy is to carry out a preorder traversal of the tree, but to enter the subtree rooted at a node only if the length of the path from the root to this node is shorter than *best*. We shall assume that the tree is represented by its Knuth transform.

Prog. 1.5 is a preorder generator, but it does not entirely suit our purpose. First, we need to be able to make "shortcuts" in the traversal, bypassing on occasion the traversal of an entire subtree. Second, we have to maintain the length of the current subpath, and, when we backtrack in the tree, this length needs to be adjusted. The first adaptation is easily made: if there is to be no traversal of a subtree of the original tree (left subtree of the transform), do not execute the statement

$$node := left(node) \tag{3.4}$$

The second problem is tougher. Suppose we keep all partial path lengths on a stack. Let $k_p$ denote the length of the path from root to node $k$. Then, in terms of the tree on the left of Fig. 2.1, as we carry out the traversal, the stack of path lengths would hold $(1_p)$, $(1_p, 2_p)$, $(1_p, 2_p, 4_p)$, $(1_p, 2_p, 4_p, 12_p)$, $(1_p, 2_p, 4_p, 12_p, 18_p)$, $(1_p, 2_p, 4_p, 12_p)$, $(1_p, 2_p, 4_p)$, $(1_p, 2_p)$, $(1_p, 3_p)$, and so forth. It is easy enough to tell when to push down a path length -- this is done whenever a node has a left child in the Knuth transform. The difficult part is knowing when and how much to pop up. For example, in the tree of Fig. 3.6 we would go from a stack containing $(1_p, 2_p, 3_p, 4_p, 5_p)$, to a stack containing

($1_p$, $2_p$) alone.

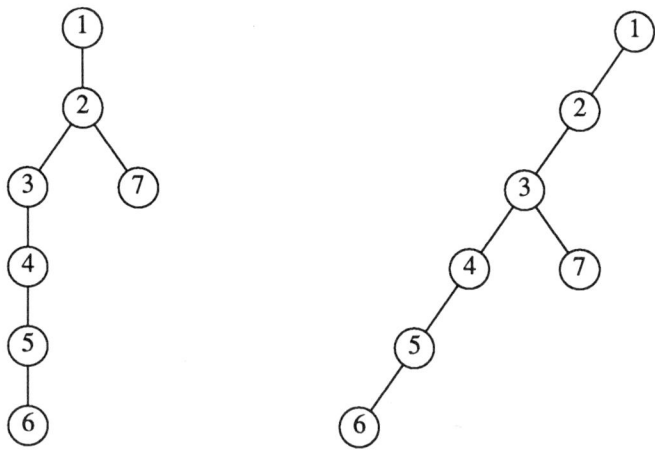

Fig. 3.6 -- A very slender tree and its Knuth transform

The solution is to push down the length of the partial path to the *parent* of a node when the node itself has a right sibling, or, in terms of the Knuth transform, when the node has a right child, and to pop up when all children of a node have been dealt with, which, in terms of the Knuth transform means that there is no further right child to consider. This is the basis of Prog. 3.4. A good feature of this solution is that the stack of lengths of partial paths is maintained outside the preorder generator. The only change to the generator is the introduction of a changing argument *enter* -- normally this argument is true, but it is false when the traversal of the subtree of the node that was last delivered is to be suppressed. Statement (3.4) then becomes

**if** *enter* **then** *node*:= *left(node)*

**else** *node*:= *newtree*

where *newtree* is a binary tree function that returns an empty binary tree. This change considerably increases the versatility of generator *preorderT*.

The test component for the shortest path problem is so primitive that it does not pay to code it as a separate routine. Prog. 3.4, which finds the length of the shortest path, has the test built in.

*stack*:= *newstack*;

*best*:= *verylargenumber*;

*pathlength*:= 0;

*enter*:= true;

*preorderT*(*pathtree, enter*, -1) <*arclength, tag*>;

**if** *tag* = F **then** ERROR MESSAGE; (* *pathtree* is empty *)

**while** *tag* ≠ F **do begin**

    *preorderT*(*pathtree, enter*, -1) <*arclength, tag*>;

    *enter*:= true;

    *newlength*:= *pathlength* + *arclength*;

    **if** *tag* = R **or** *tag* = B **then** (* node has siblings *)

        *stack*:= *push*(*stack, pathlength*);

    **if** *tag* = R **or** *tag* = T **then** (* node is terminal *)

        *best*:= *min*(*best, newlength*);

    **if** *tag* = B **or** *tag* = L **then**

        **if** *newlength* > *best* **then begin**

            *enter*:= false;

            **if not** *emptystack*(*stack*) **then begin**

                *pathlength*:= *read*(*stack*);

                *stack*:= *pop*(*stack*);

            **end**

```
            end
        else
            pathlength:= newlength;
        if tag = T or tag = R then
            if not emptystack(stack) then begin
                pathlength:= read(stack);
                stack:= pop(stack);
            end
    end
```

Prog. 3.4 -- A program for the shortest path in a tree

## 3.4 THE QUEENS PROBLEM REVISITED

Every solution of the $n$-queens problem has to be a permutation of the set $\{1, 2, ..., n\}$. If the configuration generator were to produce partial permutations, we would have a more efficient program -- for example, the number of permutations of eight elements is only $8! = 40{,}320$. Again, a single test could reduce this number by cutting off a large chunk of the space of candidate solutions. Thus, since the partial permutation

$$\boxed{1\,|\,2\,|\phantom{x}|\phantom{x}|\phantom{x}|\phantom{x}|\phantom{x}|\phantom{x}}$$

cannot lead to a solution of the 8-queens problem, $6! = 720$ of the 40,320 permutations will not have to be generated.

Consider the case $n = 4$. Fig. 3.7 shows one half of a tree in which every path from the root to a terminal node represents a permutation of $\{1, 2, 3, 4\}$. The half-tree represents all permutations that start with 1 or 2. Now, when the partial permutations are submitted to the test routine, it rejects (blocks) those in which two queens share the same diagonal. The half-tree with the blocked permutations is shown as Fig. 3.8. If, instead of Prog. 3.3, we were to use a generator of partial permutations, test

$$\forall\, t:\ 1 \leq t \leq k-1:\ (\text{not } Q(i,t)) \tag{3.5}$$

of Expression (3.2) would have to be shifted into the generator. However, we can do without an explicit test by making sure that all the configurations we generate are partial permutations.

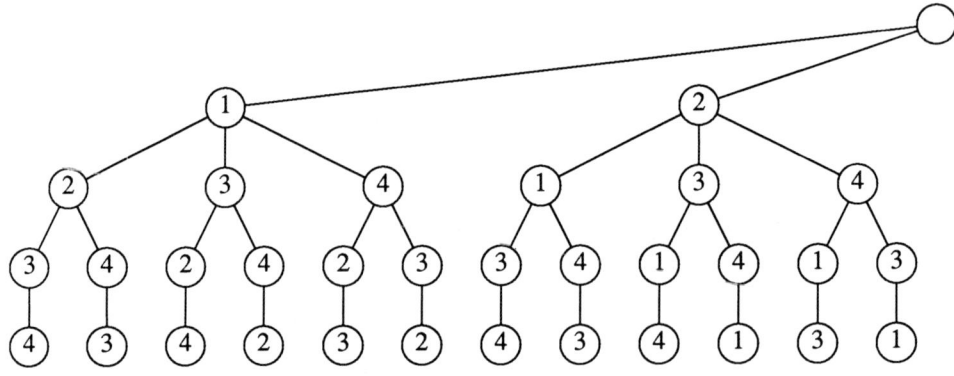

Fig. 3.7 -- Partial tree of permutations of {1, 2, 3, 4}

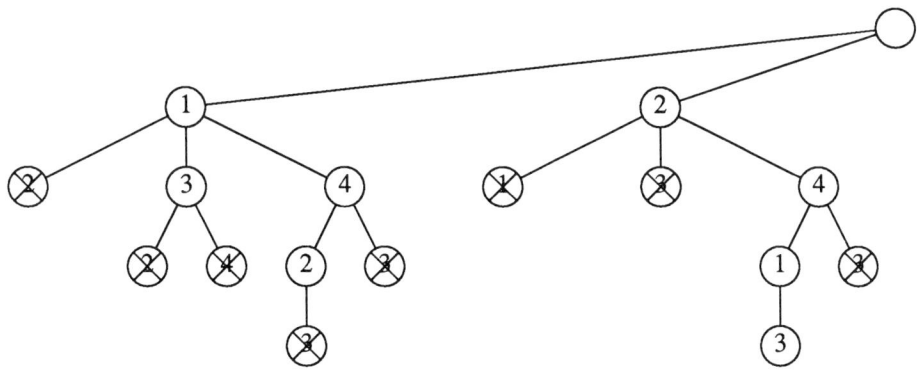

Fig. 3.8 -- Partial tree for the 4-queens problem

The generation of partial permutations raises two problems. First, how does one tell efficiently whether an element being considered for the next position in a partial permutation is not already used up? Second, how does one prevent a partial permutation from being generated more than once? A solution is to maintain two arrays. For example, in generating permutations of {1, 2, ..., 8}, as for the 8-queens problem, one array holds the partial permutation, say

| 2 | 7 | 3 | 8 |   |   |   |   |

and the other is a directory that indicates whether an element is part of the partial permutation, here

| F | T | T | F | F | F | T | T |

Now, in extending the partial permutation 2738, we pick the smallest element for which the directory entry is F, namely 1. The arrays become

| 2 | 7 | 3 | 8 | 1 |   |   |   |

| T | T | T | F | F | F | T | T |

But 27381 is not a "good" partial permutation for the 8-queens problem (the queens in columns 3 and 5 lie on the same diagonal), and the 1 is replaced by the next element greater than 1 for which the directory entry is F, which in this case is 4. The arrays change to

| 2 | 7 | 3 | 8 | 4 | | | |

| F | T | T | T | F | F | T | T |

Since 27384 is not a good partial permutation either, we try 27385 and 27386, again with no success. The directory indicates that 7 and 8 are already used up somewhere in the partial permutation. Moreover, on backtracking to the fourth position of the permutation, we find that all elements have now been tried here. Hence the next partial permutation to be investigated is 274.

## 3.5 MORE PROBLEMS BASED ON PERMUTATIONS

The traveling salesperson problem can be stated as follows. Given $n$ cities 1, 2, ..., $n$, a traveling salesperson is to start out from city 1 and return to city 1 after having visited each of cities 2, 3, ..., $n$ exactly once, in such a manner that the total distance traveled is a minimum. The possible tours when $n = 4$ are shown in Fig. 3.9.

Chap. 3]  The generate-and-test paradigm  119

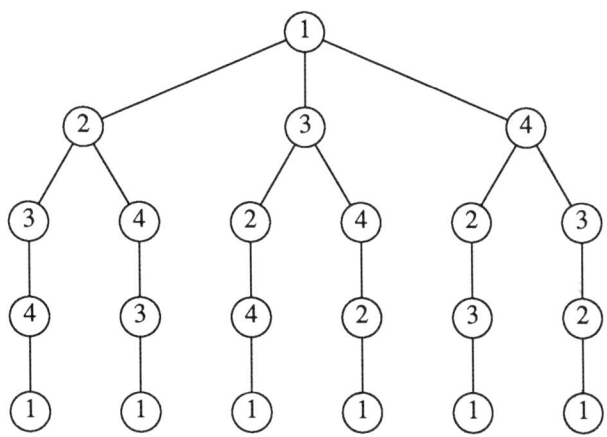

Fig. 3.9 -- Possible tours of traveling salesperson on four cities

We have here a problem that is a composite of those investigated in Sections 3.3 and 3.4. What matters are the permutations of $\{2, 3, ..., n\}$, but, once the total length of a complete tour has been determined, any partial tour that is as long or longer is not to be considered further. Hence we are again interested in partial rather than complete permutations of $\{2, 3, ..., n\}$.

We shall investigate a variant of the traveling salesperson problem, known as the assembly line problem. An assembly line is to produce $n$ different models. The cost of retooling for model $j$ after a production run of model $i$ is $c_{ij}$, and the initial cost of tooling up for model $j$ is $c_{0j}$. The $n$ models should be produced in a sequence that minimizes costs. Table 3.1 shows the tooling costs for the production of three models, and Fig. 3.10 is a tree showing the sequences in which the three models can be produced, together with the cumulative tooling costs for each sequence.

|   | j |   |   |
|---|---|---|---|
| i | 1 | 2 | 3 |
| 0 | 14 | 5 | 8 |
| 1 | - | 1 | 9 |
| 2 | 1 | - | 8 |
| 3 | 8 | 2 | - |

Table 3.1 -- Tooling costs for an assembly line

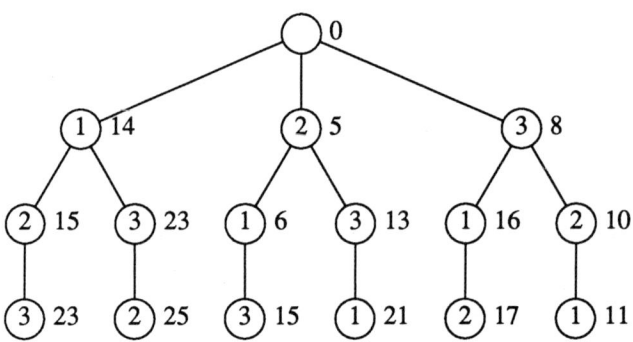

Fig. 3.10 -- Cumulative costs for the 3-model problem of Table 3.1

In analogy with the approach of Section 3.3, the sequence leading up to a node is to be extended only if the cumulative cost of this sequence is not as high as a reference cost (the cost of the cheapest total sequence found thus far, which, as in Prog. 3.4, is initialized to a very large number). In terms of Fig. 3.10, we have to consider sequences (partial permutations) 1, 12, 123, 13, 2, 21, 213, 23, 231, 3, 31, 32, 321. The sequences can be interpreted as arising from a partial preorder traversal of the tree of Fig. 3.10. This strategy is known as *depth-first*.

An alternative is a *best-cost* strategy, defined as follows. At each node selected for processing, take all arcs to the next lower level in the tree and compute the cumulative costs of these nodes. Then select the node with lowest over-all cost as the one to be processed next. The first node selected for processing is the root of the tree. In terms of Fig. 3.10, we would consider sequences 1, 2, 3, 21, 23, 213, 31, 32, 321.

The advantage of the depth-first strategy is its simplicity: the partial permutation are generated in a well defined order, and we showed in Section 3.4 how to generate these partial permutations by use of two arrays. Under the best-cost strategy we would expect to generate fewer partial permutations, but the generation of these partial permutations would be a more complicated process. We would have to store all the partial permutations that could be extended further in a priority queue ordered on the cumulative costs associated with the partial permutations. The heap that we introduced in Section 1.3 can serve as a priority queue. Here the heap would be an array of ordered pairs <cumulative cost, partial permutation>. After storage of the first three items into the heap, it has the appearance

[<5, 2>, <14, 1>, <8, 3>].

After selection of node 2 on level 1 as the next node to be processed, the heap reduces to

[<8, 3>, <14, 1>],

and after the processing of this node the heap becomes

[<6, 21>, <13, 23>, <8, 3>, <14, 1>].

Next the partial permutation 21 is selected for expansion. The cumulative cost of sequence 213 is 15, and this is saved as a tentative solution. The heap is now

[<8, 3>, <13, 23>, <14, 1>],

the sequence with cost 8 is selected for processing, and this continues until the heap has been emptied or the cumulative cost of the top entry in the heap is found to be at least as high as the reference cost.

The depth-first and best-cost strategies can be regarded as two ends of a spectrum of strategies. Depth-first is the easiest to implement, but best-cost makes better use of the information already gathered. The *branch-from-newest-active-node* strategy is just one of the hybrids that combine features of depth-first and best-cost. Under this strategy, at each node selected for processing, take all arcs to the next lower level in the tree, and compute the cumulative costs. Then select the node with the lowest cumulative cost *of these nodes* as the one to be processed next. When the entire subtree has been dealt with, back up in the tree, and select a low-valued node. In terms of Fig. 3.10, partial permutations would be considered in the order 1, 2, 3, 21, 23, 213, 231, 31, 32, 321.

No matter what the strategy, the traveling salesperson problem is hard, in the following sense. Although this has not been proven, it is suspected that in some instances the time to solve the problem must depend exponentially on the number of cities. Approximate solutions for which the difference from the exact solution is within a known bond can be found in time that has a polynomial dependence on the number of cities.

## 3.6 AND ONCE MORE THE QUEENS PROBLEM

The classical approach to the solution of combinatorial problems in operations research and computer science has been to generate a solution or a partial solution and test that it satisfies a criterion such as (3.2). In artificial intelligence, on the other hand, one might examine several alternative partial solutions, and extend the partial solution that holds greatest promise to lead to a complete solution.

Suppose that in attempting to solve the eight queens problem we have already placed three queens, and are now to place the fourth queen. If the three queens are represented by the partial permutation 135, then we could extend this to 1352, 1354, 1356, 1357, and 1358. However, if we look at the influence of the three already placed queens on the columns to the right of them, as shown in the lefthand diagram of Fig.3.11, we see that the fourth queen can go only in row 2, row 7, or row 8. The righthand diagram of Fig. 3.11 is a digitized representation of the lefthand diagram -- the number in a square gives the count of the queens that threaten this square in a "forward" sense.

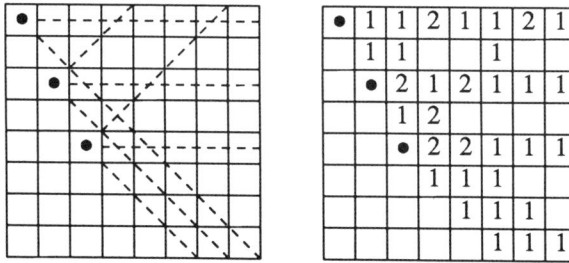

Fig. 3.11 -- The forward influence of three placed queens

However, the three permissible placements of the fourth queen are not equally likely to lead to a solution (actually none can be extended into a solution). Fig. 3.12 shows the forward influence patterns after the fourth queen has been added. We see that partial permutation 1352 cannot lead to a solution because every square in column 6 is under threat. This leaves partial permutations 1357 and 1358. Under 1357 eight squares in the rightmost four columns of the board are not being threatened; under 1358 there are nine such squares. Hence 1358 is a more promising partial solution.

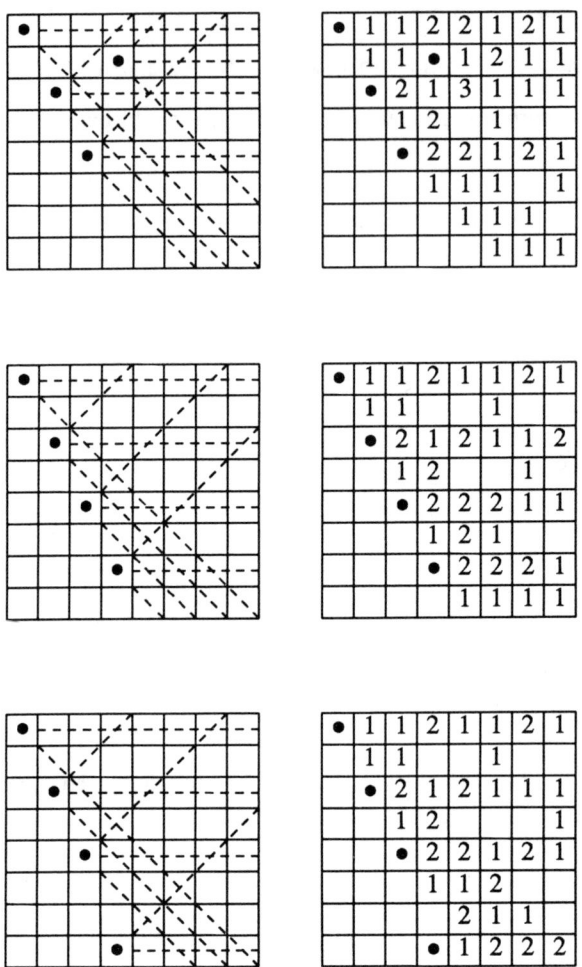

Fig. 3.12 -- Placements of the fourth queen

This forward exploration is costlier than the standard depth-first backtracking approach. First, a digitized representation of the forward influence pattern of the placed queens has to be maintained. On placing a queen, the pattern is adjusted by incrementing counts on the influence lines of the queen; on removing a queen the counts are decremented. Further, on selecting 1358 for the partial solution to be extended next, we cannot just forget 1357 -- this partial solution has to be preserved in a priority queue. Our criterion of choosing a partial solution that leaves more squares safe from attack is a *heuristic*, that is, a rule of thumb for deciding which among several alternatives is more likely to lead to a goal. We note again that 1358 does not lead to a solution. On the other hand, under 1586, which does lead to the solution of Fig. 3.2, only eight squares in the four rightmost columns are not under threat, as shown in Fig. 3.13.

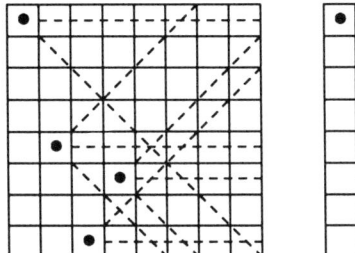

Fig. 3.13 -- Toward the solution shown in Fig. 3.2

An interesting aspect of the partial solution of Fig. 3.13 is that a complete solution can be obtained from it at once. There is only one unthreatened square in column 7. Hence, if there is to be a solution based on 1586, it has to take the form 1586**2*. But then only one square is safe in column 5, and only one square in column 6, giving 1586372*. The only possibility for column 8 is 4, and the result is 15863724. This suggests another heuristic, which is to place a queen in the column that contains the fewest safe squares. Unfortunately the use of this heuristic further complicates the representation of the problem. It also illustrates a fairly general phenomenon: the more complicated the heuristic, the more difficult it becomes to keep the phases of the generate-and-test paradigm separate.

## 3.7 THE A*-ALGORITHM

Let us look again at the traveling salesperson problem of Section 3.5. Suppose we use the best-cost strategy to solve a 20-city problem, and at some stage in the process have a partial tour of nine cities of length 30 units and a partial tour of five cities of length 28 units. The best-cost principle requires us to extend the 5-city partial tour, although for this tour we still have 15 cities to visit before returning to the start. The slightly longer 9-city partial tour leaves us with only 11 additional cities to visit, and it could well be that this partial tour leads to the solution. Best-cost strategy is based entirely on knowledge of the region of the space of potential solutions that has already been explored -- no consideration is given to the unexplored part.

In the approach to the 8-queens problem illustrated by Fig. 3.12 we were looking forward, and estimating our chances of future success in terms of the number of safe squares. Such looking forward is the basis of the $A^*$-algorithm. We shall discuss this algorithm in terms of a search for the best path from a start node to a goal node. However, before we do so, we have to introduce firm definitions.

Let $G = <A, R>$ be a (directed) graph, where $A$ is a nonempty set of nodes, and $R \subseteq A \times A$ is a set of arcs. With each $<i, j> \in R$ associate a non-negative cost (or weight, or length) $c_{ij}$. Given a path $(n_1, n_2, n_3, ..., n_k)$ in $G$, the cost (weight, length) of the path is

$$c_{n_1 n_2} + c_{n_2 n_3} + \cdots + c_{n_{k-1} n_k}.$$

A unique node $s \in A$ is the start node of $G$. We consider a process called *graph search*, or *graph exploration*, in which paths are built up from the start node $s$. Graph search is made up of *node expansions*. Given node $n$, node $m$ belongs to the successor set of $n$ if and only if $<n, m> \in R$. Now, given path $(s, ..., n)$, the expansion of node $n$ is the generation of a path $(s, ..., n, m)$ for every node $m$ in the successor set of node $n$. A search discipline or search strategy determines the order in which the nodes of $G$ are expanded. An *uninformed* search is unaffected by the part of the graph that has not yet been explored. Both depth-first and best-cost searches are uninformed. An *informed* search makes use of knowledge about the problem domain to guide the search into more promising regions of the search space. For example, the search for a solution of the *n*-queens problem as discussed in Sections 3.1 and 3.4 was uninformed, but the search of Section 3.6 was informed.

The selection of the next node to be expanded is to be determined by a function $f$, defined on set $A$. Let $X \subseteq A$ be the set of nodes that have not yet been expanded. Then the next node to be expanded is to be that $n \in X$ for which $f(n)$ is a minimum. For the traveling salesperson problem on four cities graph $G$ is the tree of Fig. 3.9, and for best-cost strategy $f(n)$ is the cost of the path from root $s$ to the tree node $n$. Note that $f(s) = 0$. It is important to distinguish here between the graph of the cities, which has only four nodes, and the graph of Fig. 3.9, which represents our search space as a tree of 22 nodes.

In the $A^*$-algorithm the node selection function $f$ has two components:

$$f(n) = g(n) + h(n), \tag{3.6}$$

where $g(n)$ is the length of the best currently known path from $s$ to $n$, and $h(n)$ is an estimate of the length of the shortest path from $n$ to a goal node. Actual lengths, unknown to begin with, shall be denoted by $f^*$, $g^*$, and $h^*$.

In all our applications $G$ is a tree, in which case there can be just one path from $s$ to any other node of $G$, which means that when a node $n$ has been expanded, $g^*$ is known for all the nodes in the successor set of $n$. We regard the application of the $A^*$-algorithm as an instance of backtracking in the sense of the our definition of backtracking in Section 3.2. Although this definition is very liberal, it still requires that the next node to be expanded be selected from the successor set of a node already expanded. Hence we can rewrite (3.6) as

$$f(n) = g^*(n) + h(n). \tag{3.7}$$

Function $h$ is the carrier of heuristic information, and its definition will be influenced by the problem domain. For the traveling salesperson problem on $k$ cities, a tour through node $n$ is made up of a known segment $(1, ..., n)$, having length $g^*(n)$ and consisting of, say, $t$ arcs, and a forward segment of which we know only that it consists of $(k - t)$ arcs. However, we can assume that the arcs in the forward segment have approximately the same length as the average length of arcs in the known segment, namely $g^*(n)/t$, and we put

$$\begin{aligned} f(n) &= g^*(n) + g^*(n)\frac{k-t}{t} \\ &= \frac{k}{t} g^*(n). \end{aligned} \tag{3.8}$$

The $f$ values corresponding to the partial tour lengths of 28 and 30 units, introduced at the beginning of this section, are $(20/4)\times28 = 140$ and $(20/8)\times30 = 75$, respectively. This means that the $A^*$-algorithm will extend the 9-city partial tour first.

## 3.8 A CASE STUDY: DIAGNOSTIC INFERENCE

Diagnosis is the identification of the underlying causes for the observed behaviour or properties of a system. For the most part diagnosis is undertaken when the system is faulty. Although most investigations have been in the context of medical diagnosis, a need for fault diagnosis can arise in many areas. For example, abnormally low temperature readings in a house could be attributed to a broken furnace, abnormally cold weather, abnormal heat loss (due to an open window, say), low thermostat setting, broken thermostat, or a combination of these causes. Let us refer to our observations of abnormality as *manifestations*, and to their possible causes as *disorders*. In medicine the manifestations consist of symptoms told by a patient, examination findings, and laboratory results; the disorders are diseases. In this section we shall study diagnostic inference as formulated by James Reggia and his associates.

Formally, a diagnostic problem $P$ is the quadruple $<D, M, S, K>$, where $D = \{d_1, ..., d_s\}$ is a finite universe of disorders, $M = \{m_1, ..., m_t\}$ is a finite universe of manifestations, and $S \subseteq M$ is the set of manifestations actually present for this diagnostic problem. Relation $K \subseteq D \times M$ represents diagnostic knowledge: $<d_i, m_j> \in K$ means that $d_i$ can cause $m_j$. Let us define two set-valued total functions:

$$man: D \longrightarrow M\text{-set}, \quad man(d_i) = \{m_j \mid <d_i, m_j> \in K\};$$
$$causes: M \longrightarrow D\text{-set}, \quad causes(m_j) = \{d_i \mid <d_i, m_j> \in K\}.$$

Here $M$-set and $D$-set represent the power sets of $M$ and $D$, respectively. For any $X \subseteq D$, the composite set of manifestations corresponding to the set of disorders $X$ is the distributed union of the images of elements of $X$ under $man$:

$$man(X) = \bigcup man(d_i).$$

Similarly, for any $Y \subseteq M$,

$$causes(Y) = \bigcup causes(m_j).$$

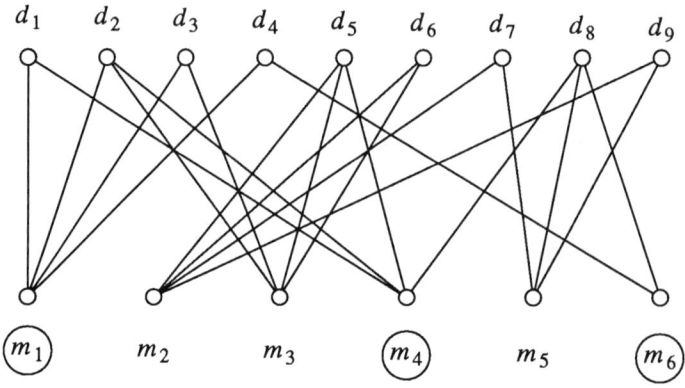

Fig. 3.14 -- Representation of a diagnostic problem

Fig. 3.14 represents a diagnostic problem based on nine disorders and six manifestations, and a diagnostic knowledge relation of 21 elements. The representation is a directed bipartite graph. The elements of $K$ should be represented by arrows. However, since all the arrows go in the same direction, from a $d_i$ to an $m_j$, the arrowheads have been omitted. The $S$ for this diagnostic problem is $\{m_1, m_4, m_6\}$, identified by circling of the appropriate elements in Fig. 3.14. Here $man(d_2) = \{m_1, m_3, m_4\}$, $causes(m_4) = \{d_1, d_2, d_5, d_8\}$, $man(\{d_1, d_5, d_8\}) = \{m_1, m_2, m_3, m_4, m_5, m_6\}$ ($= M$), $causes(\{m_2, m_4\}) = \{d_1, d_2, d_5, d_6, d_7, d_8, d_9\}$. Interpretation of $man(d_2)$: the disorder $d_2$ can cause manifestations $m_1$, $m_3$, and $m_4$, but an occurrence of a disorder $d_2$ does not necessarily have to give rise to all these manifestations. Interpretation of $causes(m_4)$: if manifestation $m_4$ is observed, then, according to our present diagnostic knowledge (as represented by relation $K$), at least one of the disorders $d_1, d_2, d_5$, and $d_8$ must be present.

Given a diagnostic problem with manifestations $S$, any subset $E$ of $D$ is a *feasible explanation* of $S$ if $S \subseteq man(E)$, that is, if the set of disorders $E$ can cause all the indicated manifestations $S$. In terms of Fig. 3.14, $causes(S) = \{d_1, d_2, d_3, d_4, d_5, d_8\}$. Of course, *causes*(S) is a feasible explanation of S, and every explanation of S has to be a subset of *causes*(S). Explanation E is *minimal* if it satisfies a given minimality criterion. Commonly the criterion is that of all the feasible explanations of S, a minimal explanation consists of the fewest disorders. This criterion will be adopted here, although situations can arise in which an explanation consisting of several disorders makes more sense than an explanation consisting of a single disorder. For example, if one feasible explanation is provided by the joint occurrence of two common diseases, and another by one very rare disease by itself, it is more likely that the patient has the two common diseases. This situation can be dealt with by assigning weights to disorders, and selecting those feasible solutions for which the sum of the weights is smallest.

The solution to a diagnostic problem $P = <D, M, S, K>$ is the set of all minimal explanations of K. No single element of *causes*(S) for the problem of Fig. 3.14 provides a feasible explanation of S, but the pairs $\{d_1, d_4\}, \{d_1, d_8\}, \{d_2, d_4\}, \{d_2, d_8\}, \{d_3, d_8\},$ $\{d_4, d_5\}, \{d_4, d_8\}$ are all feasible. Under our interpretation of a minimal explanation as the explanation with the fewest elements, these seven pairs constitute the solution to P, which we denote by *Sol*(P).

Finding an explanation for a diagnostic problem relates to the *set covering* problem: given a collection of subsets of a set R, $Q = \{R_1, R_2, ..., R_k\}$, find a collection of sets in Q such that their union is R. A solution to the set covering problem that consists of the minimal number of subsets of Q solves the *minimal* set covering problem. For example, with $R = \{1, 2, 3, 4, 5, 6\}$ and $Q = \{\{1, 3, 5\}, \{1, 4, 6\}, \{2, 3, 4\}, \{2, 6\}, \{3, 4, 6\}\}$, the minimal set covering problem has five solutions. One is $\{\{1, 3, 5\}, \{2, 3, 4\}, \{3, 4, 6\}\}$, another is $\{\{1, 3, 5\}, \{2, 6\}, \{3, 4, 6\}\}$. The set covering problem has been used to model numerous applications, such as scheduling and information retrieval. In matching up the diagnostic problem with minimal set covering, R represents S. Referring again to Fig. 3.14, we see that the $d_i$ can be identified with subsets of S: $d_1$ with $\{m_1, m_4\}$, $d_2$

with $\{m_1, m_4\}$, ..., $d_9$ with the null set. The $Q$ for the diagnostic problem of Fig. 3.14 consists of the subsets defined by the $d_i$ (but without the null set), namely $\{\{m_1, m_4\}$, $\{m_1\}, \{m_1, m_6\}, \{m_4\}, \{m_4, m_6\}\}$, and the $d_i$ corresponding to a minimal cover define minimal explanations of $S$. Thus, $\{\{m_1, m_4\}, \{m_1, m_6\}\}$ is a minimal cover, and since $\{m_1, m_4\}$ corresponds to $d_1$ or $d_2$, and $\{m_1, m_6\}$ to $d_4$, this minimal cover defines explanations $\{d_1, d_4\}$ and $\{d_2, d_4\}$.

The solution to a diagnostic problem <$D, M, S, K$> is given by all solutions to the corresponding minimal set covering problem, with an important difference. If $S \neq M$, then a minimal explanation needs to satisfy only $S \subseteq man(E)$, whereas for the set covering problem $S = man(E)$ has to hold.

In mathematics, *generators* are objects from which other objects can be built. Consider a set $T$, and a collection of its subsets $G_k = \{T_1, T_2, ..., T_n\}$, such that an element of $T$ is in at most one of the $T_i$. Then $G_k$ is a generator, and it generates the class

$$[G_k] = \{\{t_1, t_2, ..., t_n\} \mid \forall i: 1 \leq i \leq n: t_i \in T_i\}.$$

However, to avoid confusion with the generators of programming, we shall use the term *constructor* to denote the generator of mathematics. The collection $G = \{G_1, G_2, ..., G_q\}$ is a constructor set if each $G_i$ is a constructor, and no two $[G_i]$ have a member in common. The class generated by a constructor set $G$ is

$$[G] = [G_1] \cup [G_2] \cup \cdots \cup [G_q].$$

Our purpose is to express $Sol(P) = \{\{d_1, d_4\}, \{d_1, d_8\}, \{d_2, d_4\}, \{d_2, d_8\}, \{d_3, d_8\}, \{d_4, d_5\}, \{d_4, d_8\}\}$ as a constructor set on $D$. One such set is $\{G_1, G_2\}$, where $G_1 = \{\{d_4\}, \{d_1, d_2, d_5\}\}$ and $G_2 = \{\{d_8\}, \{d_1, d_2, d_3, d_4\}\}$. Another is $\{H_1, H_2, H_3\}$, with $H_1 = \{\{d_1, d_2\}, \{d_4, d_8\}\}$, $H_2 = \{\{d_4\}, \{d_5, d_8\}\}$, $H_3 = \{\{d_3\}, \{d_8\}\}$. If the set of manifestations $S$ is known from the start, it makes little difference whether $Sol(P)$ is represented explicitly as a collection of seven sets of the form $\{d_i, d_j\}$ or as a constructor set. In practice, however, $S$ is built up interactively during the solution process. An initial set of manifestations leads to the formulation of a hypothesis, a test of the hypothesis leads to further manifestations being introduced, such as when a physician prescribes new laboratory tests, this leads to the formulation of a new hypothesis, and so forth. The representation of *Sol(P)* by a constructor set becomes very convenient when a diagnostic problem is solved by means of a sequential hypothesize-and-test process.

Function *explain* of Prog. 3.5 computes a constructor set that represents all explanations of size $n$ of a diagnostic problem, that is, all explanations consisting of $n$ disorders. It is a recursive function with three arguments: *dscope*, a subset of $D$; *manifs*, a subset of $S$; and $n$. In what follows use will be made of the Pascal notation for sets: in Pascal [*d*] stands for the set {*d*}. Function *explain* may return [[]], which stands for a set that contains the null set. This return can be regarded as the base of the recursive process. The [] stands for the null set -- its return indicates that no explanation of $n$ elements exists.

**function** *explain*(*dscope*: dset; *manifs*: mset; *n*: natural): constructorset;
  **var** *L, Bcomp*: dset; *d, ref*: disorder; *A, B, C*: constructorset;
    *c*: natural; *etag, stag*: boolean;
**begin**
  *c*:= *card*(*dscope*);
  **if** $n = 0$ **and** *manifs* = [] **then**
    *explain*:= [[]]
  **else if** $n = 0$ **or** $c < n$ **then**
    *explain*:= []
  **else begin**
    *L*:= [];
    *getelement*(*dscope*, false) <*ref, ctag*>;
    *d*:= *ref*;
    **repeat**
      **if** (*man*(*d*) $\cap$ *manifs*) = (*man*(*refs*) $\cap$ *manifs*) **then**
        *L*:= $L \cup [d]$;
      *getelement*(*dscope*, true) <*d, ctag*>
    **until** *ctag*;
    *A*:= *explain*(*dscope-L, manifs, n*);
    *B*:= *explain*(*dscope-L, manifs-man*(*d*), *n*-1);
    *C*:= [];
    *getset*(*B*, false) <*Bcomp, stag*>;
    **while not** *stag* **do begin**
      *C*:= $C \cup [[L \cup Bcomp]]$;
      *getset*(*B*, true) <*Bcomp, stag*>
    **end**;

$$explain := A \cup C$$

**end**

**end** (* *explain* *)

Prog. 3.5 -- Schematic program for the computation of a constructor set

Function *explain* of Prog. 3.5 makes use of two generators, *getelement* and *getset*. In both cases the two arguments of the generator are changing arguments. When the second argument is false, the generator reads in the value supplied by the first argument, which is a set or a collection of sets, and returns the first component of this value. When the second argument is true, the generator returns the next component of its first argument. This permits the same generator to be applied sequentially to more than one structure. The function also calls *card*, which returns the cardinality of its argument, and *man*, which was defined earlier. The main activity of *explain* begins on reaching the repeat-until loop, which finds a set $L$ of disorders that cover the same subset of manifestations. Then two recursive calls are made. The first finds the constructor set $A$ from which all manifestations of size $n$ for *manifs* can be constructed in terms of *dscope*, but which do not include $L$. The second produces a constructor set for a reduced problem. Then each element of this constructor set is combined with set $L$, and the result is a constructor set $C$ from which all explanations of size $n$ for *manifs* can be constructed in terms of *dscope*, that do include $L$. The union of $A$ and $C$ is the required result.

Prog. 3.6 uses *explain* to find solutions to diagnostic problems. It calls *explain* with increasing values of $n$ until *explain* returns a non-null result.

```
function solve1(S: mset): constructorset;
    var n: natural;  C: constructorset;
begin
    n:= 0;
    C:= [];
    while C = [] do begin
        C:= explain(causes(S), S, n);
        n:= n + 1;
    end;
    solve1:= C
end (* solve1 *)
```

Fig. 3.6 -- Program for the solution of diagnostic problems

Next we use *explain* in *solve2*, which is a program for the interactive solution of diagnostic problems. Now we start with no manifestations at all, but generator *getmanif* supplies a new manifestation at every call, until there are no more manifestations. Prog. 3.7 is a schematic representation of function *solve2*. Function *quotient* takes two arguments, a constructor set $G$ and a nonempty set of disorders $D$; $quotient(G, D)$ returns a constructor set $H$ such that

$$[H] = \{E \in [G] \mid card(E \cap D) > 0\},$$

where $[H]$ and $[G]$ are the classes generated by $H$ and $G$, respectively. Function *findhypothesis*, which is called with the constructor set $quotient(hypothesis, causes(m))$ as argument, returns an element of this constructor set, that is, a constructor that represents a hypothesis. Function *causes* was defined earlier.

**function** *solve2*: constructorset;

    **var** *n*: natural; *dscope*: dset; *manifs*: mset; *m*: manifestation;

        *hypothesis*: constructorset; *mtag*: boolean;

**begin**

    *n*:= 0;

    *manifs*:= [];

    *dscope*:= [];

    *hypothesis*:= [[]];

    *getmanif* <*m, mtag*>;

    **while not** *mtag* **do begin**

        *manifs*:= *manifs* ∪ [*m*];

        *dscope*:= *dscope* ∪ *causes*(*m*);

        *findhypothesis*(*quotient*(*hypothesis*, *causes*(*m*)));

        **if** *hypothesis* = [] **then begin**

            *n*:= *n* + 1;

            *hypothesis*:= *explain*(*dscope*, *manifs*, *n*)

        **end**;

        *getmanif* <*m, mtag*>

    **end**;

    *solve2*:= *hypothesis*

**end** (* *solve2* *)

Prog. 3.7 -- Schematic program for interactive solution of diagnostic problems

Set *manifs* in *solve2* is the set of manifestations assembled up to now, and *dscope*, which is the value of *causes*(*manifs*), is the set of all disorders for which at least one manifestation is already in *manifs*. Then *hypothesis* is the constructor set for the solution of the problem $<dscope, M^*, manifs, K^*>$, which can be regarded as a reduction of the diagnostic problem $P = <D, M, S, K>$, such that (a) $dscope \subseteq D$, (b) $M^* = man(dscope)$ is evaluated with respect to the $K$ of $P$, (c) $manifs \subseteq S$, and (d) $K^* = K \cap (dscope \times M^*)$.

Let us apply *solve2* to the problem of Fig. 3.14, where we shall assume that *getmanif* delivers the manifestations in the order $m_1, m_4$, and $m_6$. Initially $n = 0$, *manifs* and *dscope* are both null sets, and *hypothesis* is a set containing the null set. On the introduction of $m_1$, *dscope* becomes $\{d_1, d_2, d_3, d_4\}$, and *hypothesis* contains just $\{\{d_1, d_2, d_3, d_4\}\}$, so that $n = 1$. Introduction of $m_4$ augments *manifs* to $\{m_1, m_4\}$, *dscope* is now $\{d_1, d_2, d_3, d_4, d_5, d_8\}$, and *hypothesis* contains $\{\{d_1, d_2\}\}$. Either $d_1$ or $d_2$ is capable of producing both the manifestations $m_1$ and $m_4$, and no other single disorder can do so. So we still have $n = 1$. Next *manifs* becomes $\{m_1, m_4, m_6\}$, *dscope* remains $\{d_1, d_2, d_3, d_4, d_5, d_8\}$, and *hypothesis* now represents the solution of $P$. Now $n = 2$ because no single disorder can give rise to all three manifestations. We saw earlier that the constructor set representing the solution need not be unique, and which constructor set is generated by *solve2* will depend on the order in which processing of the components of various data objects is carried out. One possibility is for *hypothesis* to contain the three families of sets $\{\{d_1, d_2\}, \{d_4, d_8\}\}, \{\{d_4\}, \{d_5, d_8\}\}$, and $\{\{d_3\}, \{d_8\}\}$.

# 4

# Implementation of Generators

Suppose the design of a generator-based program has been completed. For the implementation of the program we have two options: choose a language in which generators can be directly implemented, or simulate generators in a language that does not provide them. The first section of this chapter deals with the second option. The rest is devoted to programming systems that provide generators. In this our emphasis is on the programming language Icon, but the survey of Icon is not a complete guide to Icon programming; we merely wish to create enough interest in the language so that some readers will want to turn to more thorough sources.

## 4.1 SIMULATION OF GENERATORS

Some constructs of programming languages, such as go to statements and global variables have been rightfully indicted as harmful. They should be avoided because they make it difficult to reason about programs, or they may reduce the reusability potential of the software in which they appear. But they are not evil. For example, given a clear indication of the purpose of each global variable, and a guarantee that the global variable is used for this purpose alone, there is nothing wrong in the disciplined use of global variables. Similarly, in program development by transformations, some of the later transforms may well contain go to statements. Here the point is that a user wishing to know the purpose of a program or wishing to reason about the program would consult a high-level version of the program. For example, a user will come to a better understanding of preorder traversal of binary trees by looking at *pretraverse1* (Prog. 1.6) rather than *pretraverse4* (Prog. 1.9). Prog. 1.9 is not there to be looked at, but to force a compiler into an efficient implementation -- this program is conceptually closer to its machine language translation than to Prog. 1.6.

Taking this a step further, the fact that the design of a program has been expressed in terms of generators does not mean that program quality would be seriously jeopardized if the generators were converted to function or procedure subprograms. Consider Prog. 1.1, a generator of Fibonacci numbers. In order to convert this generator to a function, variables *fibminus1* and *fibminus2* have to be made global, and a comment to this effect should be included with the text of the subprogram. The comment is to assist in reuse -- if the subprogram is copied into another program, one has to make sure that the global variables are shifted as well. Another comment should be attached to the declaration of these global variables stating that their purpose is to preserve data between calls to the generator of Fibonacci numbers -- this is to prevent the use of the global variables for any other purpose. The conversion of Prog. 1.1 results in Prog. 4.1, where the additional global variable *first* distinguishes between the first and later invocations of *fibonacci*.

**function** *fibonacci*: natural;

(* this function makes use of global variables *fibminus1*, *fibminus2*,

and *first* -- *first* has to be initialized to true before the first

invocation of *fibonacci* *)

**var** *t*: natural;

**begin**

  **if** *first* **then begin**

    *t* := 1;

    *fibminus2* := 0;

    *fibminus1* := 1;

    *first* := false

  **end**

  **else begin**

    *t* := *fibminus1* + *fibminus2*;

    *fibminus2* := *fibminus1*;

    *fibminus1* := *t*;

  **end**;

  *fibonacci* := *t*

**end** (* *fibonacci* *)

Prog. 4.1 -- Simulation of a generator of Fibonacci numbers

The approach of Prog. 4.1 works well if only one instance of the generator is required. When there is need for more than one instance, then it becomes necessary either to create a separate function or procedure for each instance, or preserve data between calls by passing the data to and from the subprogram as arguments. In the latter case the heading of Prog. 4.1 becomes

**function** *fibonacci*(**var** *fibminus1, fibminus2*: natural; **var** *first*: boolean): natural;

and different instances of *fibonacci* are simulated by defining appropriate sets of actual arguments corresponding to *fibminus1, fibminus2*, and *first*.

## 4.2 AN OVERVIEW OF ICON

Specialized programming languages were being developed in the 1950s in parallel with the early general purpose high level languages Fortran and Algol60. One such language, Comit, was designed for the processing of text strings. In a series of refinements Comit evolved into Snobol4, and Snobol4 into Icon. Icon is a very useful language for applications such as stylistic analysis of literary works, symbolic mathematics, or automated program transformation. It is also a powerful general purpose language, but the specialized requirements of string processing detract somewhat from its general usefulness. For example, the flexibility of having an object "32" interpreted as a string of two characters in one context and as an integer in another is bought at the cost of having no type declarations. As a consequence beginning Icon programmers experience much frustration in debugging. However, the availability of generators more than balances the features one may perceive as deficiencies.

The components of an Icon program are declarations and expressions, where declarations provide information for the compiler, but expressions are executable code. The execution of an expression results in a value. However, some expressions, known as conditional expressions, may succeed or fail. A conditional expression has a value only if it succeeds. Since the boolean data type does not exist in Icon, an expression such as

$$x := a < b \tag{4.1}$$

cannot assign a boolean value to $x$, but it still makes perfect sense. Given that variables $a$ and $b$ have values 10 and 15, respectively, the expression on the right of the assignment operator succeeds. If a binary comparison expression succeeds, it takes the value of the expression on the right of the comparison operator, which here is the value of $b$. The assignment itself has a dual nature: the entire assignment expression (4.1) takes on the value 15, and the value 15 becomes bound to variable $x$. Here the value of (4.1) fizzles out, so to speak, but we could have, for example, used (4.1) as an argument in a procedure call. If the values of $a$ and $b$ had been 15 and 10, respectively, expression $a < b$ would have failed, and, since $a < b$ would not then have a value, (4.1) would have failed as a whole, leaving $x$ with its old value. In most programming languages only one of the comparison operators $<$ and $>$, say, is needed, but in Icon, because $(a > b)$ and $(b < a)$ have different values, both are necessary.

The interpretation of (4.1) given above is not entirely correct. Some expressions produce values, others produce variables. The result of (4.1) is actually the variable $x$. Often it does not matter whether we interpret the result as a variable or as its value, but in some instances it does. For example, one can assign to a variable, but not to a value. Hence

$$(x := a < b) := q \tag{4.2}$$

would be invalid if $x := a < b$ resulted in a value. As it is, if $a$ is smaller than $b$, then the value of $q$ is assigned to $x$, but $x$ keeps its old value if $a$ is not smaller than $b$.

In most programming languages control is based on the truth or falsity of boolean expressions. In Icon it is in general based on success or failure of conditional expressions, and there is no boolean data type. However, there is a similarity between booleans and the success-failure aspect of Icon expressions. Thus, if expression *expr* succeeds, the expression **not** *expr* fails, and if *expr* fails, then **not** *expr* succeeds. Icon provides a null value, and this is the value of **not** *expr* when it succeeds. In most contexts the use of null values is erroneous. For example, $c + $ **not** $(a < b)$ is a meaningless expression. If $a < b$ succeeds, then **not** $(a < b)$ fails, the addition cannot take place, and the entire expression fails. If **not** $(a < b)$ succeeds, then its value is null, and use of the null value in an arithmetic expression is interpreted as an error. A conjunction of expressions, denoted by

$$expr_1 \ \& \ expr_2 \qquad (4.3)$$

succeeds only if both $expr_1$ and $expr_2$ succeed. The result of (4.3) is the result of $expr_2$. Icon does not provide for disjunction of expressions.

The two basic ways in which the sequential execution of a program can be modified are selection and iteration. In Icon selection takes the form of if-then-else (or just if-then) and case constructs. For example,

$$\textbf{if} \ expr_1 \ \textbf{then} \ expr_2 \ \textbf{else} \ expr_3 \qquad (4.4)$$

results in $expr_2$ if $expr_1$ succeeds, but in $expr_3$ if $expr_1$ fails. The effect of (4.2) can be achieved in a simpler and clearer fashion by the use of an if-then:

$$\textbf{if} \ a < b \ \textbf{then} \ x := q$$

In keeping with the statement of purpose made in the introduction to this chapter, we shall not provide a complete guide to Icon. In particular, since the case construct can be easily simulated by nested if-then-else expressions, there is no need to discuss case expressions.

The looping construct

$$\textbf{while} \ expr_1 \ \textbf{do} \ expr_2 \qquad (4.5)$$

provides one example of iteration. First *expr*₁ is evaluated. If the evaluation succeeds, then *expr*₂ is evaluated, and subsequently *expr*₁ is evaluated again, which keeps the process going. If, however, at any stage *expr*₁ fails, then *expr*₂ is not evaluated, and the loop terminates. The expression

$$\textbf{until not } expr_1 \textbf{ do } expr_2$$

is equivalent to (4.5). This illustrates a general feature of Icon -- its vocabulary could be significantly reduced without reducing the expressive power of the language.

Another iterative construct is

$$\textbf{every } expr_1 \textbf{ do } expr_2 \qquad (4.6)$$

which evaluates *expr*₂ for every result produced by *expr*₁. The *expr*₁ of (4.6) is a generator, and we postpone discussion of the every-do loop to the next section.

Instead of being a simple expression, *expr*₂ of (4.4), (4.5), and (4.6), and *expr*₃ of (4.4) can be a compound expression. A compound expression is constructed by enclosing a sequence of simple expressions in braces, as in

>    *linecount*:= 0
>    **while** *line*:= *read*() **do** {
>        *write*(*line*)
>        *linecount*:= *linecount* + 1
>    }

The purpose of this program segment is to read an input file line by line, write out each line, and maintain a count of the lines. When the input file has been exhausted, the Icon built-in input function *read* fails, and the loop terminates.

If the expression **next** is reached in the execution of a loop, then control passes immediately to the expression that follows the **while** or **every** of this loop, but if the expression **break** is reached, an immediate exit from the loop takes place. Because the $expr_1$ in (4.5) or (4.6) can represent quite an extensive computation, the **do** $expr_2$ may not be needed, and it can be omitted. For example,

$$\textbf{while } write(read())$$

is equivalent to

$$\textbf{while } line := read() \textbf{ do } write(line)$$

There is also a do-forever construct:

$$\textbf{repeat } expr \qquad (4.7)$$

evaluates *expr* repeatedly, irrespective of whether *expr* succeeds or fails. Execution of a repeat-loop can be terminated by means of a **break**. Of course,

$$\textbf{while } 5 = 5 \textbf{ do } expr$$

is an effective simulation of (4.7).

An Icon program is made up of procedures. One of the procedures must be named *main*, and execution of the program starts with this procedure. Procedure *main* may be the entire program, as in

**procedure** *main*()
    *write*("This is an Icon program")
**end**

which causes the string "This is an Icon program" to be written out.

In some programming languages the distinction between a function and a procedure is that a function call results in a value being bound to the name of the function, while a call to a procedure results in no such binding. In Icon every procedure call is an expression that succeeds or fails, and, if it succeeds, this expression has a value. Hence the conventional distinction between functions and procedures does not arise, and in Icon the term function is applied to built-in procedures (of which there are 44). In other words, all Icon subprograms are procedures, with a special subclass being known as functions.

If an expression that is used as an argument to a procedure fails, then the procedure call fails as well. Sometimes it is convenient to make a procedure fail explicitly. This can be achieved by means of the **fail** expression, which causes a return from a procedure without a value. The other way to return is by means of the **return** expression. Execution of

**return** *expr*

results in evaluation of *expr*, and a return to the calling procedure with *expr* as the value of the procedure call. The bare

**return**

returns the null value. Note that there is a distinction between a call failing and it returning a null value. For example,

**return** 10 < 5

fails, but

**return not** (10 < 5)

returns the null value. An example of the use of **fail** is shown as Prog. 4.2, which is to count the number of zeros in a linear array of natural numbers. The Icon operator * finds the size of its operand, here the number of elements in *array*. If there is no actual array, the procedure should be undefined, which is achieved by the **fail**. Otherwise *total* is incremented by 1 each time a[k] < 1 succeeds. The symbol # indicates the start of a comment.

>**procedure** *zerocount(array)*
>    *n*:= **\****array*       # find size of *array*
>    **if** *n* = 0 **then fail**     # *array* has no elements
>    **else** {
>        *total*:= 0;  *k*:= 1
>        **while** *k* <= *n* **do** {
>            *total*:= *total* + (*a*[*k*] < 1)
>            *k*:= *k* + 1
>        }
>    }
>    **return** *total*
>**end**    # *zerocount*

Prog. 4.2 -- Count of zeros in a linear array of natural numbers

Icon procedures can be recursive. The claim is sometimes made that a recursive procedure is not as efficient as a nonrecursive procedure. This claim has only partial validity. For example, with proper use of the techniques for implementing functional programs, the recursive procedures for the traversal of binary trees or for the Towers of Hanoi problem can be as efficient as their nonrecursive counterparts. On the other hand, a recursive procedure for the Fibonacci numbers, which we give in its Icon version as Prog. 4.3, is grossly inefficient. Thus, to compute the Fibonacci number $f_5$, 15 calls are made (8 of which are with $k = 0$ or $k = 1$), and to compute the sequence $f_0, f_1, ..., f_9$, 276 calls in all have to be made to *fibonacci1*.

**procedure** *fibonacci1(k)*

    **if** *k* = 0 **then**

        **return** 1

    **if** *k* = 1 **then**

        **return** 1

    **return** *fibonacci1(k-1) + fibonacci1(k-2)*

**end**    # *fibonacci1*

Prog. 4.3 -- A recursive procedure for the Fibonacci numbers

The own variables of Algol60 are revived in Icon as so called static memory, and Icon also allows expressions to be grouped into an initial block, which is executed only once, on the first call to the procedure. Thus, Prog. 4.4, which is not a generator in our sense of the term, is fully equivalent to Prog. 1.1.

```
procedure fibonacci2()
    static fibminus2, fibminus1
    local t      # t does not persist between calls
    initial {
        fibminus2 := 0
        fibminus1 := 1
        return 1
    }
    t := fibminus2 + fibminus1
    fibminus2 := fibminus1
    fibminus1 := t
    return t
end      # fibonacci2
```

Prog. 4.4 -- A procedure for computing the Fibonacci sequence

Note that a procedure name has to be followed by a list of arguments, which may be empty, as in the case of *fibonacci2*. An Icon program must contain a procedure called *main*, and execution of the program starts in this procedure.

## 4.3 GENERATORS IN ICON

Every Icon expression can be regarded as a generator. An expression "returns" a value every time it is executed. For example, in the loop

> **while** ... ... ... **do** {
>
>   ... ... ... ... ...
>
>   ... ... ... ... ...
>
>   $x[i] := \text{limit} < j$
>
>   $i := i + 1$
>
>   $j := j + 1$
>
>   ... ... ... ... ...
>
>   ... ... ... ... ...
>
> }

the expression $\text{limit} < j$ (if it succeeds) "returns" a different value in each iteration of the loop. However, the expression has to be executed anew to get the next value. In Icon the term "generator" is reserved for expressions that produce a sequence of results in a single execution. The problem is how to access the components of this sequence. One possibility is to use the control construct **every**:

> **every** *genexpr* **do** *expr*

evaluates *expr* for every element of *genexpr*. A widely used generator schema is

> *m* **to** *n* **by** *k*

which generates the integer sequence $m, m + k, m + 2k, ..., n$. The generator can be abbreviated to *m* **to** *n*, which is equivalent to *m* **to** *n* **by** 1. For example,

> $k := 0$
>
> **every** 0 **to** 20 **by** 4 **do** $k := k + 1$

results in $k$ having the value 5. Most of the time, however, we have to bind the values produced by the generator to some variable so as to link up *genexpr* with *expr*. This is done by an assignment. Thus,

$$k := 0$$
$$\textbf{every } i := 0 \textbf{ to } 20 \textbf{ by } 4 \textbf{ do } k := k + i$$

results in $k$ having the value 60. Here we have some slight loss of the elegance that otherwise characterizes the design of Icon. This has to do with the placement of **every**. Its placement suggests that the entire generator $0$ **to** $20$ **by** $4$ is assigned to $i$, and the **every** applied to the $i$ as a generator, but what is one then to make of the $i$ in the expression $k := k + i$? The intended interpretation: for every value in $0$ **to** $20$ **by** $4$, assign this value to $i$, and then do $k := k + i$.

Generator sequences can be concatenated. For example,

$$expr_1 \mid expr_2$$

is a generator that produces the sequence defined by $expr_1$, and then the sequence defined by $expr_2$. A special case is provided by

$$\mid expr$$

For example, $\mid (1 \textbf{ to } 3)$ produces $1, 2, 3, 1, 2, 3, 1, 2, 3, \ldots$ . This is an infinite sequence, but the sequence produced by a generator can be curtailed. Thus, $\mid (1 \textbf{ to } 3) \setminus 5$ produces $1, 2, 3, 1, 2$. In general,

$$genexpr \setminus intexpr$$

where $intexpr$ has an integer value, produces at most $intexpr$ results from the sequence defined by $genexpr$.

A generator sequence of zero length fails. For example, the if-then-else expression

$$\textbf{if } \mid (1 \textbf{ to } 3) \setminus 0 \textbf{ then } count := 1 \textbf{ else } count := 0$$

assigns 0 to *count*. Some of the Icon built-in functions for string processing are generators. Thus the function *find(arga, argb)* is a generator that produces for *every* instance in which *arga* is a substring of *argb*, the character position at which the substring starts in *argb*. It is in keeping with the general Icon philosophy that *find* should fail if *arga* is not a substring of *argb*.

Now, suppose the sequence generated by *find*("a", *stringx*) is 4, 8, 12, 27, 32, 36, 41, and the conditional expression

$$find(\text{"a"}, stringx) > 20$$

is to be evaluated. There is failure with 4, but other values in the sequence are tried until there is success, or the sequence is exhausted. Here 8 and 12 result in failure as well, but the expression succeeds for 27. By coupling **every** to the conditional expression, we could, for example, count the number of substrings starting in positions greater than 20:

$$k := 0$$
**every** *find*("a", *stringx*) > 20 **do** $k := k + 1$

The components of a composite data object, such as the characters of a string *C*, or the elements of a list *C*, are generated by !*C*. Actually, depending on the context, the component generator can produce a sequence of variables or a sequence of values. As regards strings and lists, they are variables. This means that one can initiate every element of a list to zero by the expression

**every** !*mylist*:= 0

Users can define Icon procedures that act as generators. Although Prog. 4.4 shows that the program designs discussed in Chapters 1-3 could be implemented as Icon procedures that are not generators, there is greater convenience in implementing them as generators. For example, the generator of Prog. 4.5, which is equivalent to Prog. 4.4, is much more compact than Prog. 4.4.

> **procedure** *fibonacci3*()
>     **local** *fibminus2, fibminus1, t*
>     **suspend** (*fibminus2*:= 1) | (*fibminus1*:= 1)
>     **repeat** {
>         **suspend** *t*:= *fibminus2* + *fibminus1*
>         *fibminus2*:= *fibminus1*
>         *fibminus1*:= *t*
>     }
> **end**   # *fibonacci3*

Prog. 4.5 -- An Icon generator of the Fibonacci sequence

The call *fibonacci3*() returns the Fibonacci sequence. The first element computed is 1, and in the process of this computation 1 is assigned to *fibminus2*. Similarly the second element is 1, and an assignment of 1 is made to *fibminus1*. The Fibonacci recurrence is used to generate the other elements of the sequence. Of course, since the sequence is infinite, the members of the sequence are computed only as needed. But, since Prog. 4.5 returns the entire Fibonacci sequence, there is a major difference between Progs. 4.5 and 1.1. The statement

> **every** *write*(*fibonacci3*() \ 10)

causes the Fibonacci sequence to be generated, truncated to its first 10 elements, and the 10 elements written out. However, the second expression in

> **every** *write(fibonacci3()* \ 10)
>
> **every** *write(fibonacci3()* \ 10)

does not produce the next 10 elements of the Fibonacci sequence, but the first 10 elements for a second time. We need greater flexibility.

Flexibility is provided by Icon co-expressions. Although this oversimplifies matters, we can regard the creation of a co-expression from a generator by an operator **create** as the setting up of a queue that contains the elements of the generated sequence in order, and extraction of an element of this sequence by an operator @ as popping off and returning the top element of the queue -- a process called *activation* in Icon. For example,

> *fibx*:= **create** *fibonacci3()*

creates as *fibx* the Fibonacci sequence. After *fibx* has been created, the program segment

> **every** 0 **to** 4 **do** *@fibx*
>
> *k*:= 0
>
> **every** 5 **to** 20 **do** *k*:= *k* + *@fibx*

first discards $f_0, f_1, ..., f_4$, and then finds in $k$ the sum $\sum_{i=5}^{20} f_i$. The separation of the creation of a sequence from accessing of its elements by means of the @ allows Icon generator procedures to be recursive, in contrast to the generators of Chapters 1-3.

Let us now find the $k$ of expression (1.3) of Section 1.2. The following program segment will do the job

> *fiby*:= **create** *fibonacci3*()
>
> *sum*:= 0;  *k*:= 0
>
> **while** *sum*:= (*bound* > *sum* + *@fiby*) **do** *k*:= *k* + 1

The co-expressions *fibx* and *fiby* are to be regarded as instances of a generator defined by *fibonacci3*. Just as is done by *@fibx*, the co-expression *@fiby* delivers in turn $f_0, f_1, f_2, \ldots$ . In the while loop an $f_i$ is added to the sum of the Fibonacci numbers up to $f_{i-1}$. If (*bound* > *sum* + *@fiby*) succeeds, the result of the addition becomes the value of the righthand side of the assignment expression, this value is assigned to *sum*, and the loop is iterated once more.

## 4.4 BACKTRACKING AND ICON GENERATORS

Recall *stringx* of Section 4.3 in which the letter "a" was found at positions 4, 8, 12, 27, 32, 36, and 41, and suppose there is a *stringy* in which "a" occurs at positions 8, 12, 16, 22, 26, 36, 39, 46. The output produced by the expression

> **every** *write*(*find*("a", *stringx*) = *find*("a", *stringy*))

is 8, 12, and 36. Every element in the sequence generated from *stringx* has to be compared against every element in the sequence generated from *stringy*, which results here in 7 × 8 comparisons. We cannot do better than this because we cannot make any assumptions regarding the nature of the sequences (such as uniqueness of elements or ordering of elements).

The equality comparison is an instance of backtracking. Let us call *find*("a", *stringx*) the left and *find*("a", *stringy*) the right argument of the equality operator. The process starts off with evaluation of both arguments, but the left argument is evaluated first. The comparison 4:8 fails, and evaluation resumes with the generator most recently activated. This is the right argument, which produces 12, but the comparison 4:12 fails as well, and so do 4:27, ..., 4:41. At this point the right argument is exhausted, an advance is made in the left argument, and the right argument starts all over again. Comparison 8:8 succeeds, but 8:12, 8:16, etc. fail. Next 12:8 fails, 12:12 succeeds, and the only other success results from the comparison 36:36. The important characteristic of the equality test is that the individual equality comparisons are scheduled by the Icon system rather than the user. Note that the output produced by

$$write(find("a", stringx) = find("a", stringy))$$

without the **every** is just 8. In this instance the Icon system still strives to find a case that succeeds.

The equality operator is not alone in producing a sequence of results. For example,

$$(1 \text{ to } 3) + (2 \text{ to } 4)$$

generates 3 (=1+2), 4 (=1+3), 5, 4, 5, 6, 5, 6, 7. Now, if one were to define *summa* as a co-expression by means of

$$summa := \textbf{create } ((1 \text{ to } 3) + (2 \text{ to } 4))$$

a sequence of executions of @*summa* would result in the values 3, 4, 5, 4, ... .

There are two kinds of backtracking, *control* backtracking and *data* backtracking. The equality comparison discussed above is an example of control backtracking. Icon also permits data backtracking. Normally the side effects caused by the evaluation of an expression are irreversible. For example

$$i := j > k \tag{4.8}$$

makes the assignment of $k$ to $i$ only if $j > k$, but

$$(i := k) < j$$

makes the assignment of $k$ to $i$ in any case, and then tests whether $j > k$. A failure of the comparison has no effect on the assignment. Under data backtracking the assignment can be reversed, as in

$$(i \leftarrow k) < j \qquad (4.9)$$

where the <- is a reversible assignment operator. The reversible assignment occurs only if $j > k$. Although (4.8) and (4.9) have the same effect here, reversible assignment may be more convenient when expressions become complicated.

We shall now discuss a program for the 8-queens problem in Icon. In Section 3.1 we used a single vector $S$ to determine whether a queen could be placed in a particular location of a column, and, if it could, $S$ was extended. An alternative is to maintain vector $S$ as before, but to have three additional vectors that tell, for each row, each southwest-northeast diagonal, and each northwest-southeast diagonal, when it is occupied. Let us call these vectors *row*, *swne*, and *nwse*, respectively. Vector *row* has $n$ elements, and *swne* and *nwse* have $2n-1$ elements each. The advantage of this approach is that it makes it easier to implement a strategy for placing the queens that does not follow a strict left to right placement of the queens in their columns.

However, the Icon implementation of Prog. 4.6 adheres to left to right order, and, instead of maintaining an array $S$, where $S[i]$ tells in which row the queen of column $i$ is placed, there are calls to a generator $S$, where $S(i)$ returns the number of the row. The interesting feature of Prog. 4.6 is the use of reversible assignments. Clearly Prog. 4.6 is much more compact than Progs. 3.1-3.3.

```
procedure main()
    every write(S(1), S(2), S(3), S(4), S(5), S(6), S(7), S(8))
end    # main

procedure S(c)
    suspend setqueen(1 to 8, c)
end    # S

procedure setqueen(r, c)
    static row, swne, nwse
    initial {
        swne:= list(15, 0); nwse:= list(15, 0); row:= list(8, 0)
    }
    if row[r] = swne[r+c-1] = nwse[8+r-c] = 0 then
        suspend row[r] <- swne[r+c-1] <- nwse[8+r-c] <- r
end    # setqueen
```

Prog. 4.6 -- An Icon program for the 8-queens problem

The write statement in *main* succeeds only if all its arguments succeed. Consider an argument $S(c)$. This is the call to the generator $S$ for column $c$. In $S$ there is a call to *setqueen*, and the generator (1 **to** 8) in this call indicates that all 8 squares in column $c$ are to be tried. The initial part of *setqueen* creates lists (linear arrays) *swne*, *nwse*, *row*, with 15, 15, 8 elements, respectively, and initiates all the elements to zero. Note that the numbering of the *swne* diagonals starts in the northwest corner, and the numbering of the *nwse* diagonals in the northeast corner. Both numberings progress clockwise around the board. For example, the diagonals through square (1, 1) are defined by *swne*[1] and *nwse*[8], the diagonals through (1, 8) by *swne*[8] and *nwse*[1], through (8, 1) by *swne*[8] and *nwse*[15], through (8, 8) by *swne*[15] and *nwse*[8].

The square (*r*, *c*) is safe if *row*[*r*], *swne*[*r+c*-1], and *nwse*[8+*r-c*] all hold zeros, and, if this is so, the current row number is assigned to these three locations in a composite reversible assignment. Moreover, *setqueen* is also a generator, and the row number becomes part of its sequence. If next $S(c+1)$ does not succeed, execution of *setqueen*(*r*, *c*) is resumed, and this starts off by reversal of the previous assignments. Recall that *r* represents the generator (1 **to** 8).

## 4.5 THE LUCID LANGUAGE

Equations (1.1) and (1.2) of Section 1.1 define the Fibonacci numbers, but these equations can also be regarded as a program for the computation of the Fibonacci numbers in an equational programming language. If we want to find $f_4$, Equation (1.2) tells us that we have to compute $f_2$ and $f_3$ first, and so forth. We get

$$\begin{aligned} f_4 &= f_2 + f_3 \\ &= (f_0 + f_1) + (f_1 + f_2) \\ &= (f_0 + f_1) + (f_1 + (f_0 + f_1)) \\ &= (1 + 1) + (1 + (1 + 1)) \\ &= 5 \end{aligned}$$

Of course it makes no difference in what order Equations (1.1) and (1.2) have been written down.

An entity may maintain the same value throughout a computation, or the value may change. For example, the constant 3 remains unchanged, and so do the variables *k* and *m* during the computation of the sum $\sum_{i=k}^{m} i \times i$, but the variable *i* assumes values *k*, *k*+1, ...,

$m$. The problem is how to express the change in the value of $i$ from $k+j$ to $k+j+1$ equationally. In the equational programming language Lucid the problem is solved by the introduction of a time scale $t_0, t_1, t_2, \ldots$ . With respect to this time scale $i$ has the value $k$ at time $t_0$, the value $k+1$ at time $t_1$, and so forth. The corresponding values of the sum are $0, k^2, k^2 + (k+1)^2, \ldots$ . Why this sequence starts with zero will be explained later.

The time scale is not explicit. Instead, it is implied by positions of values in data streams. We have already seen data streams in Icon: the expression |1 stands for the infinite sequence $<1, 1, 1, \ldots>$. In Lucid the expression 1 by itself represents $<1, 1, 1, \ldots>$. As regards our summation, we have $k$, $m$, $i$, and *sum* representing data streams

$<k, k, k, \ldots>$,

$<m, m, m, \ldots>$,

$<k, k+1, k+2, \ldots>$,

$<0, k^2, k^2 + (k+1)^2, k^2 + (k+1)^2 + (k+2)^2, \ldots>$.

A language for programming in terms of such data streams has to allow for the initiation of $i$ from $k$, changes in the data streams for $i$ and *sum*, and the "termination" of the computation after $i$ has reached the value $m$. We shall see how Lucid provides these features by examining a program segment for the computation of $\sum_{i=k}^{m} i \times i$, but first we need to look at some simpler examples.

When binary operators are applied to data streams, the results are new data streams obtained by applying the operators to corresponding elements of their arguments. Thus $x + y$, where $x$ is $<x_1, x_2, x_3, \ldots>$ and $y$ is $<y_1, y_2, y_3, \ldots>$, results in $<x_1 + y_1, x_2 + y_2, x_3 + y_3, \ldots>$. Suppose $s$ is sequence $<4, 8, 12, 16, 20, 24, \ldots>$ and $t$ is sequence $<1, 4, 9, 16, 25, 36, \ldots>$, then $s + t$ results in $<5, 12, 21, 32, 45, 60, \ldots>$ and $s < t$ results in $<$false, false, false, false, true, true, $\ldots>$. The sequence $<1, 2, 3, 4, \ldots>$ is created by

**first** $i = 1$;

**next** $i = i + 1$

The **first** operator binds the sequence $<1, 1, 1, ... >$ to $i$. Operator **next** converts a sequence $<s_1, s_2, s_3, ... >$ into $<s_2, s_3, ... >$. Here its use is to be interpreted as saying that the stream of values of $i$ at $t_1, t_2, ...$ is to be computed from the stream of values of $i$ at $t_0, t_1, ...$ and the stream $<1, 1, 1, ... >$. The result is $<1, 2, 3, 4, ... >$. In Icon recursion is made possible by separating the creation of a sequence from extraction of elements from the sequence by means of the @ operator. Here a kind of recursion is introduced by the use of the **next** operator.

Our next example is the program segment

**first** $x = 1$;

**next** $x = y$;

**first** $y = 1$;

**next** $y = x + y$

This segment produces as $x$ the stream $<1, 1, 2, 3, 5, ... >$ and as $y$ the stream $<1, 2, 3, 5, 8, ... >$, where sequence $x$ should by now be quite familiar.

Let us now examine the Lucid code for the summation example:

$k = $ **first** *input*;

$m = $ **first next** *input*;

**first** $i = k$;

**next** $i = i + 1$;

**first** *sum* $= 0$;

**next** *sum* $= $ *sum* $+ i \times i$;

*output* $= $ *sum* **as soon as** $i > m$

The input to this program segment is provided by a data stream *input*, of which we know that the first two elements are 2 and 5, but not what the other elements are. Thus *input* is <2, 5, ?, ?, ?, ... >. Then **first** *input* is <2, 2, 2, ... >, which is bound to k, **next** *input* is <5, ?, ?, ... >, but **first** applied to this is <5, 5, 5, ... >, and this stream is bound to m. The actual computation is illustrated by Table 4.1. The condition $(i > m)$ holds for the first time at $t_4$. At this time the value of *sum* with respect to $t_4$ has been computed from values of *sum* and *i* with respect to $t_3$, and the stream <54, 54, 54, ... > is bound to *output*.

|  | $t_0$ | $t_1$ | $t_2$ | $t_3$ | $t_4$ | $t_5$ | ... |
|---|---|---|---|---|---|---|---|
| k | 2 | 2 | 2 | 2 | 2 | 2 | ... |
| m | 5 | 5 | 5 | 5 | (5) | 5 | ... |
| i | 2 | 3 | 4 | 5 | (6) | 7 | ... |
| sum | 0 | 4 | 13 | 29 | (54) | 90 | ... |

**Table 4.1** -- Data streams for the computation $\sum_{i=k}^{m} i \times i$ with $k = 2, m = 5$.

Given streams *x* and *y*, $s = x$ **followed by** *y* is an abbreviation for

**first** $s = x$;

**next** $s = y$

If $x$ is <5, 6, 7, ... > and $y$ is <1, 2, 3, ... >, then $x$ **followed by** $y$ represents <5, 1, 2, 3, ... >. Now, suppose stream $x$ is <8, 7, 9, 6, 10, 5, 11, 4, ... > and stream $y$ is <8, 8, 8, ... >. Then

if $x < y$ then $x$ else $y$

defines the stream <8, 7, 8, 6, 8, 5, 8, 4, ... >. The $i$th element of this stream is obtained by comparing the $i$th elements of $x$ and $y$. If the element in the $x$ stream is smaller, then this element goes into the result stream; otherwise the element from the $y$ stream contributes to the result stream.

A data stream can be defined in a manner similar to the definition of an Icon generator. For example, the following Lucid generator defines the Fibonacci sequence <1, 1, 2, 3, 5, ... >:

    *fibonacci* **where**

        *fibonacci* = 1 **followed by** 1 **followed by** *fibonacci* + **next** *fibonacci*;

    **end**

Since *fibonacci* is <1, 1, 2, 3, 5, ... >, and **next** applied to it is <1, 2, 3, 5, ... >, the application of operator + results in the stream <2, 3, 5, 8, ...>. Observe how recursion is being achieved here by means of the **next** operator.

Lucid is not just a programming language, but also a formal system for proving properties of Lucid programs. Since a program is simply an unordered set of equations that define data streams, properties of its result stream can be derived by means of rules of the formal system.

## 4.6 UNIX PIPES AND LAZY EVALUATION

Unix is a trademark of AT&T Corporation that stands for an operating system used on a large variety of computers. An interesting feature of Unix is the use of *pipes*. The manuscript of this book was prepared using Unix facilities, and at one point I typed

refer syms ch3 | pic -Tpsc | deqn -Tpsc | ditroff -Pps2 -ms -o1-5

The vertical bar | is the pipe operator, which, used in the context

*proc1* | *proc2*

indicates that the standard output of *proc1* is to be the standard input of *proc2*. An expression that consists of alternating process designators and pipe operators is called a *pipeline*.

Returning to our example, the "refer syms ch3" appends my file of the text of Chapter 3 to a file that defines special mathematical symbols for the use of process deqn. The composite file is sent to process pic, which converts descriptions of diagrams in the Pic language into instructions for the Postscript output preparation system. The file next goes to process deqn (a local version of the Unix eqn), where mathematical expressions are made ready for the printer. The final stage is a text formatting process in which ditroff (local version of troff) formatting instructions and predefined macro-instructions identified by the option -ms are used to produce a formatted output file. The file is to be printed on the device identified by -Pps2. However, the -o1-5 indicates that only the first five pages are to be printed.

Each of the processes can be regarded as a generator that receives as input the output of the preceding process (if any) and sends its output on to then next process. For example, deqn gets its input from pic, and its output is handed on to ditroff. Now, the manuscript of Chapter 3 has 35 pages, but only the first five pages were to be printed.

Consequently, if the processes were applied blindly in left to right order, with no concern for what is needed in the end, the efforts of pic and deqn would be expended in vain on pp. 6-35 of the manuscript.

Efficiency is achieved by borrowing the concept of *lazy evaluation* from functional programming. There it has to do with evaluation of arguments in function application. Suppose a function $F$ is defined by

**function** $F(x, a, b)$

**if** $x > 0$ **then** $a$ **else** $b$

where it is stated that the value of $F$ is $a$ if $x > 0$ and $b$ otherwise, and we make the call

$$F(q, G(q), H(q))$$

Under *greedy* evaluation, both $G(q)$ and $H(q)$ are evaluated before $F$ is called. But with our example $H(q)$ does not have to be evaluated when $q > 0$, and $G(q)$ does not have to be evaluated when $q \leq 0$. Under lazy evaluation only those arguments are evaluated that are actually needed for the evaluation of $F$. Lazy evaluation is essential in programming with generators because the sequences they generate may be infinite.

## 4.7 DATA FLOW COMPUTATION

Data flow diagrams can be used for conceptual modeling during software design, or they can represent execution patterns of a program. The two types of diagrams are quite different -- one relates to an attitude to modeling, the other to an execution technology.

Fig. 4.1 shows a diagram of four processes that comprise a high level model of a system for filling orders. The interpretation of boxes, bubbles, and arrows is the same as in Fig. 2.4 of Section 2.5. No data stores are shown in Fig. 4.1 because it is assumed that each process has access to a centralized data base. For example, process OAcc, which determines whether an order can be accepted, needs to get credit ratings of customers from the data base, and the order completion process OCom requires inventory information. (The other two processes create a delivery order for the warehouse and do the billing.)

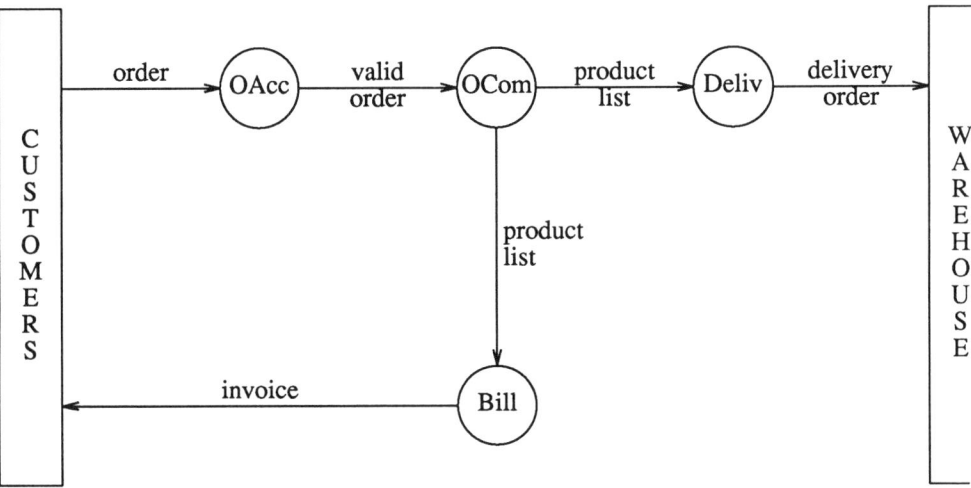

Fig. 4.1 -- High level data flow diagram of order processing

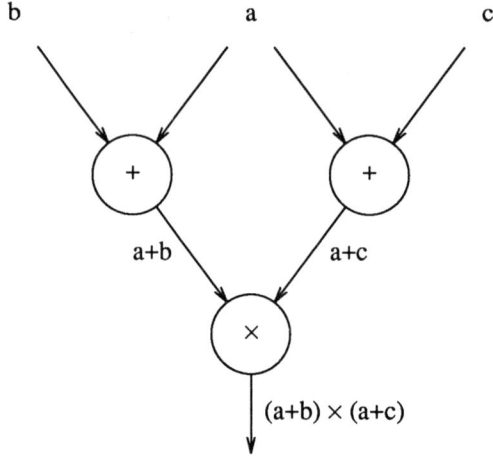

Fig. 4.2 -- Data flow diagram for evaluation of (a+b) × (a+c)

Fig. 4.2 also shows data flows and processes. However, here the data flows are transfers of single values, the processes are register-level arithmetic operations, and the concern is the design of parallel computer architectures to facilitate fast execution of computation such as the (a+b) × (a+c) defined by Fig. 4.2.

Despite their differences, Figs. 4.1 and 4.2 have much in common. Broadly speaking, a representation of a computation can emphasize data flow or control flow. Under control flow the ordering of operations has to be explicitly indicated by a programmer. Under data flow the ordering of operations is implicit and need not be deterministic. For example, Fig. 4.1 tells that, for a particular purchase order, processes Deliv and Bill cannot start before process OCom is completed, but, once OCom is completed, either of Deliv and Bill can be executed before the other, or they can proceed in parallel. Similarly, as long as all input data are available, Fig. 4.2 indicates no preference for one or other of the two additions.

We noted in Section 4.6 that the processes that are combined in Unix pipelines can be regarded as generators. The spelling checker of Fig. 2.4 can be easily implemented as a Unix pipeline. The processes of Fig. 4.1 can also be regarded as generators, but here we have an extension of the basic pipeline concept in that the output of a process can be the input of more than one process, as in the case of "product list" of Fig. 4.1.

A further categorization of data flow computations partitions them into data driven and demand driven. A data-driven computational process depends on availability of input data. In this, the earlier model of data flow computation, streams of data are *pushed* through an interconnected network of bubbles. A spelling checker that follows the design of Fig. 2.4 provides a particularly telling example of data-driven computation. Demand-driven computation is *goal directed*. An example is the computation of a Fibonacci number by application of the recurrence scheme (1.1-1.2). If $f_4$ is the goal, then (1.1) establishes $f_2$ and $f_3$ as subgoals, the subgoals of $f_2$ are $f_0$ and $f_1$, and so forth, as shown at the beginning of Section 4.5. Another example is the text formatting pipeline of Section 4.6 where data are *pulled* in from a preceding process only to the extent needed by its successor process. Here the goal is established by the limited output option -o1-5.

# Appendix A

## Exercises

This appendix contains 31 exercises, which relate to Chapters 1-3, and to Section 4.1. They all require a fairly substantial amount of work. For Exercises 1.3, 2.5, and 3.7 the indicated references may have to be consulted.

1.1. Design a generator for prime numbers. The efficient generation of prime numbers is a complicated task -- your generator need not be very efficient. A reasonably efficient method to determine whether $n$ is prime is to test remainders of the division of $n$ by all primes less than or equal $\sqrt{n}$. Note that 1 is not a prime, but that 2 is a prime.

1.2. The binomial coefficients can be generated by means of the recurrence relation

$$C(n,r) = C(n-1,r) + C(n-1,r-1), \quad n \geq 0, 0 < r \leq n,$$

with $C(n, 0) = 1$ for all $i$. Design a generator that returns, for $n = 0, 1, 2, \ldots$, the largest of the binomial coefficients $C(n, 0), C(n, 1), C(n, 2), \ldots, C(n, n)$.

1.3. Smoothsort, defined in reference [Di82], derives from heapsort, but is more efficient when the data are nearly sorted to begin with. Is there any advantage to implementing smoothsort by a generator? If so, design the generator.

1.4. Try to improve Prog. 1.12.

1.5. Develop a generator for postorder traversal of binary trees by transforming the recursive formulation given at the beginning of Section 1.8. Be sure to include a demonstration of the correctness of the generator.

2.1. The telegram problem is a well-known variant of the text formatting problem of Section 2.2. A program is to process a stream of telegrams received from an input device (generator) as a sequence of words made up of letters and digits, with words separated by blanks. A telegram ends with the word ZZZZ. The input is terminated by an empty telegram, that is, a telegram consisting of zero or more blanks followed by ZZZZ. Processing consists of counting the words to be charged, checking for overlong words, and assembling a neat listing of the telegram. The words STOP and ZZZZ are not to be charged, and words more than 12 characters long are considered overlong. The listing is to consist of the text of the telegram, accompanied by a count of the words to be charged, and a message indicating the presence of an overlong word. Use this specification, which derives from [He72], to design a telegram formatter. Since the specification is incomplete, make your own assumptions where necessary.

2.2. Given a sequence $a_1 a_2 \cdots a_n$. A subsequence $a_i \cdots a_k$ is a plateau if (i) $k > i$, (ii) for all $j$ such that $i \le j < k$, $a_j = a_{j+1}$, (iii) $i \ne 1$ implies $a_i \ne a_{i-1}$, and (iv) $k \ne n$ implies $a_k \ne a_{k+1}$. The length of plateau $a_i \cdots a_k$ is $k-i+1$. A maximal plateau is a plateau with length no smaller than that of any other plateau in the sequence. Design a program that finds the length of a maximal plateau in a sequence that is delivered to this program by a generator, one element at a time. Also write a precise specification of the generator.

2.3. Prove by an informal argument the correctness of a two-way merge program based on Table 2.1.

2.4. The generator of Prog. 2.3 returns some values more than once. Modify it so that each value is returned exactly once, and make appropriate changes to Prog. 2.4 and to Table 2.1. Has this modification been worthwhile?

2.5. Design a generator for the Hamming sequence, defined as follows: (i) $f_1 = 1$; (ii) for all i, if $f_i$ is in the sequence, then so are $2 \times f_i$, $3 \times f_i$, $5 \times f_i$; (iii) the sequence contains no additional values, that is, no value divisible by a prime number greater than 5; (iv) no value is to be generated twice -- for example, although 10 arises as a consequence of both $2 \times f_i$ and $5 \times f_i$, it is to appear only once in the sequence. (You may refer to [Ma80] for a discussion of this problem.)

2.6. Complete the verification of the file update problem of Section 2.4.

2.7. Given sequences of numbers $a_1 a_2 \cdots a_m$ and $a_1 a_2 \cdots a_n$ such that $\forall i: 1 \leq i < m: a_i \leq a_{i+1}$ and $\forall j: 1 \leq j < n: b_j \leq b_{j+1}$. Adapt the merge program of Section 2.5 to determine whether these two ascending sequences have the same elements. For example, 1222334899 and 1123489 do have the same elements.

2.8. Prove by an informal argument that Prog. 2.10 produces a list of all text words not found in the dictionary, and that the list contains only such words.

2.9. Prove by an informal argument that Progs. 2.12 and 2.13 are a correct implementation of multiplication of sparse matrices.

3.1. The conventional n-queens problem requires that $n$ queens be placed on an $n \times n$ board so that they do not threaten each other. The safe minimal coverage problem requires that the least number of queens be placed so that every free square on the board is threatened by at least one queen, but the queens do not threaten each other. The lefthand drawing of Fig. A.1 shows a solution of the safe minimal coverage problem for a $4 \times 4$ board. Design a program that solves the safe minimal coverage problem.

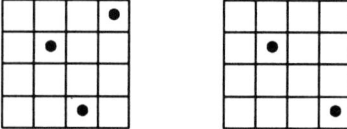

Fig. A.1 -- Variants of the 4-queens problem

3.2. The minimal coverage problem differs from the safe minimal coverage problem by allowing queens to threaten each other. The righthand drawing of Fig. A.1 shows a solution of the minimal coverage problem for a $4 \times 4$ board. Design a program that solves the minimal coverage problem.

3.3. In chess a rook threatens any piece in its row or column, and a bishop threatens any piece on the diagonals passing through its position. The $n$-rooks problem consists of placing $n$ rooks on an $n \times n$ chess board so that they do not threaten each other. The bishops problem consists of placing the maximum number of bishops on the board so that they do not threaten each other (for $n > 2$, this number is greater than $n$). Investigate these two problems. Also formulate and discuss a minimal coverage problem for bishops.

3.4. Develop a program for the $n$-queens problem based on the discussion of Section 3.4.

3.5. Design a program for the traveling salesperson problem using depth first strategy. (In developing your design keep in mind Exercise 3.6).

3.6. Convert your program for the traveling salesperson problem of Exercise 3.5 to one that uses best-cost strategy and the $A^*$-algorithm as discussed at the end of Section 3.7.

3.7. Our concern has been primarily with partial permutations. Design a generator of complete permutations. You may find it helpful to consult reference [Se77].

3.8. Given a permutation $a_1 a_2 \cdots a_n$ of $\{1, 2, ..., n\}$. This permutation is a derangement if $\forall i: 1 \le i \le n: a_i \ne i$ holds. Devise a generator for derangements. (There are approximately $n!/e$ derangements, where $e$ is the base of natural logarithms.)

3.9. If five beads, $a, b, c, d, e$, are strung on a wire, and the ends of the wire joined up, there is no distinction between the ordering *abcde, cdeab,* and even *edcba*. When $n$ beads are so strung on a wire, the number of distinct permutations, which are known as rosary permutations, is ½ $(n-1)!$. Design a generator for rosary permutations.

3.10. A dinner party consists of $n$ ($n \ge 3$) married couples, who are to be seated at a round table in such a way that no husband sits next to his wife. This is known as the problem of menages. Design a program that finds all valid seating arrangements. (Hint: each solution corresponds to a permutation $a_1 a_2 \cdots a_n$ of $\{1, 2, ..., n\}$ such that the three numbers in each column of the table

| 1 | 2 | ... | $n-1$ | $n$ |
| 2 | 3 | ... | $n$ | 1 |
| $a_1$ | $a_2$ | ... | $a_{n-1}$ | $a_n$ |

are different.)

3.11. Develop a program for the $n$-queens problem based on the approach illustrated by Fig. 3.12 in Section 3.6.

3.12. Design a program for the $n$-queens problem based on the heuristic discussed at the end of Section 3.6, namely that a queen be placed in the column with fewest unthreatened squares. Note that a "permutation tree" such as Fig. 3.7 no longer models the problem, and that influence lines have to be plotted in both "forward" and "backward" directions.

4.1. Implement Prog. 2.11.

4.2. Implement and test the matrix multiplication scheme of Progs. 2.12 and 2.13.

4.3. The efficiency of the approaches to the $n$-queens problem as discussed in Sections 3.1, 3.4, and 3.6 can be measured in two ways: by determination of the collective count of the number of queens placed on the board, and by the time to solve the problem. Implement the designs of Section 3.1, and Exercises 3.4, 3.11, and 3.12 with a provision for the two efficiency measures, and discuss the relationship of the two measures.

4.4. A better understanding of the differences in the approaches to the $n$-queens problem as discussed in Sections 3.1, 3.4, and 3.6 can be obtained by examinimg the board patterns defined by counts of the number of times a queen is placed on a particular square. For this you will need to have done Exercise 4.3, and will now need to modify the programs of that exercise.

4.5. Implement the diagnostic inference program of Section 3.8.

# Appendix B

Bibliographic notes

These bibliographic notes do not aim at providing extensive lists of references for any of the topics raised in this book. They are intended merely to lead the reader to more detailed coverage of a topic or a different viewpoint from that expressed here, or to attribute some of the material I have used. As regards my own work, this book is an elaboration of [Be88]. My commitment to the view that application software should be regarded as primarily consisting of data types made up of sets and functions was made clear in [Be86], but the most forceful arguments for this view are to be found in [Pa72] and [Pa72a].

Generators can be implemented in any language that provides a coroutine facility or something similar. A general discussion of coroutines and their implementation is to be found in [Ma80]. The languages CLU and Alphard are described in [Li81] and [Sh81], respectively. There are many texts on Modula-2 and Ada, but Chapter 16 of [Bu89] is an explicit introduction to coroutines in Modula-2, and [Bu87] can be consulted on the relevant aspects of Ada.

The solution of the Fibonacci recurrence scheme (1.1-1.2) is derived in numerous books on difference equations or analysis of algorithms -- see, for example, [Kn68]. Heapsort was published as [Fl64]. For smoothsort, a sorting algorithm that combines some features of heapsort with those of quicksort see [Di82]. A survey and classification of binary tree traversals is to be found in [Be86a]. The use of tags with a generator was introduced in [Be88]. The Knuth transform is defined on p.333 of [Kn68].

Verification of programs by logical proofs is surveyed in [Gu89]. The distinction between logical and mathematical proofs of programs has been discussed in [Cu83]; there is little else in the literature on mathematical proofs of programs. However, the cleanroom approach to programming [Mi86, Mi87] can be regarded as a methodology for carrying out such proofs. Some representative texts on testing: [My79], [Be83], [Ou86]. On software reliability, which provides the theoretical support for verification by testing, see [Mu87].

Transformational development of software by application of correctness-preserving transformations has been surveyed in [Pa83]. For the transformational development of a suite of programs in the domain of context-free languages see [Pa86]. Another interesting example of of a program developed by transformations is given in [Br81]. These two studies were performed in the framework of the Munich CIP project, using the wide spectrum language CIP-L [Ba85a] and the transformation system CIP-S [Ba87]. Another example of transformational programming is presented in [Ba81]; the environment in which this work was carried out is described in [Ba85]. Much of the work on program transformation has related to functional programming -- Chapter 4 of [He87] is a fine introduction. The informal approach to transformational development, exemplified by our Sections 1.6-1.8, owes much to program development by stepwise refinement [Wi71].

The motivation for introducing tags was provided by a problem I faced in the development of a package of programs for critical path analysis. A detailed discussion of the intermeshed traversals of Prog. 2.1 can be found in [Be80]. The requirements for the text formatter of Section 2.2 are taken from the problem set for the Fourth International Workshop on Software Specification and Design [Ha87]. The predicative specification of the text formatter as given in Section 2.2 here was first published in [Be90]. The similar telegram problem of Exercise 2.1 was introduced in [He72]; it is discussed in some detail in [Ma80] and in Sections 5.3.2 and 5.3.5 of [Po86].

The two-way merge of Section 2.3, and updating of files of Section 2.4 are the two major examples of [Be88]. One way of looking at these examples is to regard a generator as having state, and a tag as defining the state. The use of state indicators has been studied in [He75], [At79], [Ju80], [He82]. Updating of files with a view similar to that expressed in Section 2.4 is discussed in [Di76] and [Dw81].

The use of data flow diagrams (as in Fig. 2.4) is discussed in [De78], [Ga79], and [Yo89]. For AVL trees see, for example, [Ho76]. A discussion of coroutines centered on the problem of doubled characters was carried on in [Gr77], [Ly78], [Ja78], [Be78], and [Le78]. The problem of doubled characters is discussed in [Ma80] as well, where there is also a discussion of the Hamming sequence of Exercise 2.5. For computation of the Hamming sequence as the processing of data streams see pp.180-183 of [Ch88]. The interpretation of matrices as functions, as in Section 2.7, dates at least as far back as [Mc62].

The queens problem has been a very popular example for illustrating different attitudes to programming -- of the works listed in our bibliography for their relevance to some other topic, at least [Ba81], [Bu82], [He80], [Gr83], [Pe84], and [Wi71] deal with this problem. It seems that [Go65] contains the first discussion of computational aspects of the queens problem. This reference also mentions the safe minimal coverage problem of Exercise 3.1. Backtracking in general is introduced in Chapters 7 and 8 of [Ho78]; it is looked at from four different viewpoints in [Ge76], [Li79], [Pu81], and [Ma87]. The shortest path problem of Section 3.3 is discussed in [Li79]. Methods for generating permutations are surveyed in [Se77], but for a method that is relevant to the generation of partial permutations see [Er87].

The approach to the queens problem taken in Section 3.6 has been suggested in

[Pe84]. This is also a good reference for the A*-algorithm. Machine learning is introduced in [Mi83] and [Mi86]. The case study of Section 3.8 follows [Re85] and [Re85a]; [Pe87] reports on extensions of the earlier work.

For a general introduction to Icon see [Gr83]. However, [Gr81] is more detailed on generators, particularly on how Icon generators relate to similar features in other languages, and on the implementation of Icon generators. The more recent [Gr88] adds little that is new. Generators similar to those of Icon have been added to C [Bu82]. Prog. 4.6 derives from [Gr83]. See Chapter 4 of [He87] on how to improve the efficiency of Prog. 4.3 in the context of functional programming. The original Lucid articles are [As76] and [As77]; a thorough coverage is provided in [Wa85]. Lucid has been extended into a language for real-time computing -- see [Fa86].

The origin of Unix pipes is traced in [Ri80]. Pipelined networks are described in Section 8.3.2 of [Ch88], but to understand this material one has to read earlier parts of this reference (which would be time very well spent). A construct similar to Unix pipes is described in [Ra83]. On lazy evaluation see, for example, [He80]. Data flow computing is surveyed in [Sh85]; [Ve86] is a more specialized survey of architectures of computers designed for data flow computing. The use of a particular model of data flow computation in automatic programming is described in [Ba88].

# Appendix C

## Bibliography

[As76]   Ashcroft, E.A., and Wadge, W.W., Lucid -- a formal system for writing and proving programs. *SIAM J. Computing* **5** (1976), 336-354.

[As77]   Ashcroft, E.A., and Wadge, W.W., Lucid, a nonprocedural language with iteration. *Comm. ACM* **20** (1977), 519-526.

[At79]   Atkinson, L.V., Pascal scalars as state indicators. *Software--Practice and Experience* **9** (1979), 427-431.

[Ba81]   Balzer, R., Transformational implementation: an example. *IEEE Trans. Software Eng.* **SE-7** (1981), 3-13.

[Ba85]   Balzer, R., A 15 year perspective on automatic programming. *IEEE Trans. Software Eng.* **SE-11** (1985), 1257-1268.

[Ba85a]  Bauer, F.L., et al., *The Munich Project CIP, Volume I: The Wide Spectrum Language CIP-L*. Lecture Notes in Computer Science, No. 183, Springer-Verlag, Berlin, 1985.

[Ba87]   Bauer, F.L., et al., *The Munich Project CIP, Volume II: The Program Transformation System CIP-S*. Lecture Notes in Computer Science, No. 292, Springer-Verlag, Berlin, 1987.

[Ba88]   Barstow, D., Automatic programming for streams II: transformational implementation. *Proc. 10th Internat. Conf. Software Eng.*, Computer Society Press, Washington, DC, 1988, 439-447.

[Be78]     Bezivin, J., Nebut, J.-L., and Rannou, R., Another view of coroutines. *ACM SIGPLAN Notices* **13**, 5 (May 1978), 23-35.

[Be80]     Berztiss, A.T., Depth-first K-trees and critical path analysis. *Acta Informatica* **13** (1980), 325-346.

[Be83]     Beizer, B., *Software Testing Techniques*. Van Nostrand, New York, 1983.

[Be86]     Berztiss, A.T., Data abstraction in the specification of information systems. *Proc. IFIP World Congress 86*, pp.83-90.

[Be86a]    Berztiss, A., A taxonomy of binary tree traversals. *BIT* **26** (1986), 266-276.

[Be88]     Berztiss, A., Programming with generators. *Softw. Pract. Exp.* **18** (1988), 73-81.

[Be90]     Berztiss, A., Formal specification methods and visualization. In *Principles of Visual Programming Systems* (S.-K. Chang, Ed.), Prentice-Hall, Englewood Cliffs, New Jersey, 1990, pp.231-290.

[Br81]     Broy, M., and Pepper, P., Program development as a formal activity. *IEEE Trans. Software Eng.* **SE-7** (1981), 14-22.

[Bu82]     Budd, T.A., An implementation of generators in C. *Computer Lang.* **7** (1982), 69-87.

[Bu87]     Burns, A., Lister, A.M., and Wellings, A.J., *A Review of Ada Tasking*. Lecture Notes in Computer Science, No. 262, Springer-Verlag, Berlin, 1987.

[Bu89]     Budgen, D., *Software Development with Modula-2*. Addison-Wesley, Wokingham, UK, 1989.

[Ch88]     Chandy, K.M., and Misra, J., *Parallel Program Design - A Foundation*. Addison-Wesley, Reading, MA, 1988.

[Cu83]     Culik, K., and Rizki, M.M., Logic versus mathematics in computer science education. *ACM SIGCSE Bulletin* **15**, 1 (Feb. 1983), 14-20.

[De78] DeMarco, T., *Structured Analysis and System Specification*. Yourdon Press, New York, 1978.

[Di76] Dijkstra, E.W., *A Discipline of Programming*. Prentice-Hall, Englewood Cliffs, New Jersey, 1976.

[Di82] Dijkstra, E.W., Smoothsort, an alternative for sorting in situ. *Sci. Computer Prog.* **1** (1982), 223-233 (errata: *Sci. Computer Prog.* **2** (1982), 85).

[Dw81] Dwyer, B., One more time--how to update a master file. *Comm. ACM* **24** (1981), 3-8.

[Er87] Er, M.C., An efficient implementation of permutation backtracking in lexicographic order. *Computer J.* **30** (1987), 282.

[Fa86] Faustini, A.A., and Lewis, E.B., Toward a real-time dataflow language. *IEEE Software* **3** 1 (Jan.1986), 29-35.

[Fl64] Floyd, R.W., Algorithm 245: Treesort 3. *Comm. ACM* **7** (1964), 701.

[Ga79] Gane, C., and Sarson, T., *Structured Systems Analysis: Tools and Techniques*. Prentice-Hall, Englewood Cliffs, NJ, 1979.

[Ge76] Gerhart, S.L., and Yelowitz, L., Control structure abstractions of the backtracking programming technique. *IEEE Trans. Software Eng.* **SE-2** (1976), 285-292.

[Go65] Golomb, S.W., and Baumert, L.D., Backtrack programming. *J. ACM* **12** (1965), 516-524.

[Gr77] Grune, D., A view of coroutines. *ACM SIGPLAN Notices* **12**, 7 (July 1977), 75-81.

[Gr81] Griswold, R.E., Hanson, D.R., and Korb, J.T., Generators in Icon. *ACM*

*Trans. Program. Lang. Syst.* **3** (1981), 144-161.

[Gr83]  Griswold, R.E., and Griswold, M.T., *The Icon Programming Language*. Prentice-Hall, Englewood Cliffs, New Jersey, 1983.

[Gr88]  Griswold, R.E., Programming with generators. *Computer J.* **31** (1988), 220-228.

[Gu89]  Gumb, R.D., *Programming Logics*. Wiley, New York, 1989.

[Ha87]  Harandi, M.T. (Ed.), *Proc. Fourth International Workshop on Software Specification and Design*.

[He72]  Henderson, P., and Snowdon, R., An experiment in structured programming. *BIT* **12** (1972), 38-53.

[He75]  Henderson, P., Finite state modelling in program development. *Proc. 1975 Internat. Conf. Reliable Software*: SIGPLAN Notices **10**, 6 (1975), 221-227.

[He80]  Henderson, P., *Functional Programming -- Application and Implementation*. Prentice-Hall, Englewood Cliffs, New Jersey, 1980.

[He82]  Hext, J., and Hirst, S., The formal treatment of state transition tables--a tutorial. *Austral. Computer J.* **14** (1982), 1-6.

[He87]  Henson, M.C., *Elements of Functional Languages*. Blackwell, Oxford, 1987.

[Ho76]  Horowitz, E., and Sahni, S., *Fundamentals of Data Structures*. Computer Science Press, Woodland Hills, CA, 1976.

[Ho78]  Horowitz, E., and Sahni, S., *Fundamentals of Computer Algorithms*. Computer Science Press, Potomac, MD, 1978.

[Ja78]  Jacobsen, T., Another view of coroutines. *ACM SIGPLAN Notices* **13**, 4 (April 1978), 68-75.

[Ju80]  Juliff, P., Program control by state transition tables. *Austral. Computer J.* **12** (1980), 146-152.

[Kn68]  Knuth, D.E., *The Art of Computer Programming, Vol. 1 / Fundamental Algorithms.* Addison-Wesley, Reading, MA, 1968.

[Le78]  Lewis, B., Further comments on "A view of coroutines." *ACM SIGPLAN Notices* **13**, 7 (July 1978), 31-33.

[Li79]  Lindstrom, G., Backtracking in a generalized control setting. *ACM Trans. Prog. Lang. Syst.* **1** (1979), 8-26.

[Li81]  Liskov, B., et al., *CLU Reference Manual.* Lecture Notes in Computer Science, No. 114, Springer-Verlag, Berlin, 1981.

[Ly78]  Lynning, E., Letter to the editor. *ACM SIGPLAN Notices* **13**, 2 (Feb. 1978), 12-14.

[Ma80]  Marlin, C.D., *Coroutines.* Lecture Notes in Computer Science, No. 95, Springer-Verlag, Berlin, 1980.

[Ma87]  Marcus, S., Taking backtracking with a grain of SALT. *Int. J. Man-Machine Studies* **26** (1987), 383-398.

[Mc62]  McCarthy, J., Towards a mathematical science of computation. *Proc. IFIP World Congress 1962*, pp.21-28.

[Mi83]  Michalski, R.S., Carbonell, J.G., and Mitchell, T.M. (Eds.), *Machine Learning: An Artificial Intelligence Approach.* Tioga, Palo Alto, CA, 1983.

[Mi86]  Michalski, R.S., Carbonell, J.G., and Mitchell, T.M. (Eds.), *Machine Learning: An Artificial Intelligence Approach, Vol.II.* Morgan Kaufmann, Los Altos, CA, 1986.

[Mi86a]  Mills, H.D., Basili, V.R., Gannon, J.D., and Hamlet, R.G., *Principles of*

*Computer Programming, A Mathematical Approach.* Allyn and Bacon, Newton, MA, 1986.

[Mi87] Mills, H.D., Dyer, R., and Linger, R.C., Cleanroom software engineering. *IEEE Software* **4**, 5 (Sept. 1987), 19-25.

[Mu87] Musa, J.D., Iannino, A., and Okumoto, K., *Software Reliability -- Measurement, Prediction, Application.* McGraw-Hill, New York, 1987.

[My79] Myers, G.J., *The Art of Software Testing.* Wiley, New York, 1979.

[Ou86] Ould, M.A., and Unwin, C. (Eds.), *Testing in Software Development.* CUP, Cambridge, England, 1986.

[Pa72] Parnas, D.L., A technique for software module specification with examples. *Comm. ACM* **15** (1972), 330-336.

[Pa72a] Parnas, D.L., On the criteria to be used in decomposing systems into modules. *Comm. ACM* **15** (1972), 1053-1058.

[Pa83] Partsch, H., and Steinbruggen, R., Program transformation systems. *ACM Comp. Surveys* **15**(1983), 199-236.

[Pa86] Partsch, H., Transformational program development in a particular problem domain. *Sci. Computer Prog.* **7** (1986), 99-241.

[Pe84] Pearl, J., *Heuristics: Intelligent Search Strategies for Computer Problem Solving.* Addison-Wesley, Reading, MA, 1984.

[Pe87] Peng, Y., and Reggia, J.A., Diagnostic problem-solving with causal chaining. *Internat. J. Intelligent Systems* **2** (1987), 265-302.

[Po86] Pomberger, G., *Software Engineering and Modula-2.* Prentice-Hall, Englewood Cliffs, New Jersey, 1986.

[Pu81] Purdom, P.W., Brown, C.A., and Robertson, E.L., Backtracking with multilevel dynamic search rearrangement. *Acta Informatica* **15** (1981), 99-113.

[Ra83] Raoult, J.-C., and Sethi, R., Properties of a notation for combining functions. *J. ACM* **30** (1983), 595-611.

[Re85] Reggia, J.A., Nau, D.S., and Wang, P.Y., A formal model of diagnostic inference -- I. Problem formulation and decomposition. *Information Sciences* **37** (1985), 227-256.

[Re85a] Reggia, J.A., Nau, D.S., Wang, P.Y., and Peng, Y., A formal model of diagnostic inference -- II. Algorithmic Solutions and Applications. *Information Sciences* **37** (1985), 257-285.

[Ri80] Ritchie, D.M., The evolution of the Unix time sharing system. In *Proc. Symp. Language Design and Programming Methodology* (J.M. Tobias, Ed.), Lecture Notes in Computer Science, No. 79, Springer-Verlag, Berlin, 1980, pp.25-35.

[Se77] Sedgewick, R., Permutation generation methods. *ACM Comp. Surveys* **9**(1977), 137-164.

[Sh81] Shaw, M., ed., *Alphard: Form and Content*. Springer-Verlag, New York, 1981.

[Sh85] Sharp, J.A., *Data Flow Computing*. Ellis Horwood, Chichester, UK, 1985.

[Ve86] Veen, A.H., Dataflow machine architecture. *ACM Comp. Surveys* **18**(1986), 365-396.

[Wa85] Wadge, W.W., and Ashcroft, E.A., *Lucid, the Dataflow Programming Language*. Academic Press, London, 1985.

[Wi71] Wirth, N., Program development by stepwise refinement. *Comm. ACM* **14** (1971), 221-227.

[Yo89]	Yourdon, E., *Modern Structured Analysis*. Yourdon Press, Englewood Cliffs, NJ, 1989.

# Index

Ada  15, 177
Algol60  15, 142, 149
Alphard  15, 177
application software  9
argument passing
    by changing value mode  21
    by fixed value mode  21
    by value mode  21
    by variable mode  21
artificial intelligence  12
assembly line problem  119
$A^*$-algorithm  126, 180
AVL tree  87, 179
backtracking  109, 127
    and Icon generators  156
    best-cost  121, 126, 127
    branch-from-newest-active-node  122
    control  157
    data  157
    depth-first  121
binary tree traversal  25, 36
binomial coefficients  171
changing value mode  21
C  180
CLU  15, 177
Comit  142
constant  13
coroutine  179
data flow computation  166, 180
    data driven  169
    demand driven  169
data flow diagram  86, 167, 168, 179
data stream  10, 12, 161
data transformer  9
    object oriented  10
    stream oriented  10

data type  11
    basic  10
    of heap  18
    of stack  25
derangement  175
device  10
diagnostic problem  128
    disorder  128
    manifestation  128
do-forever  17, 22, 51
doubled characters problem  89, 179
efficiency  35
eight-queens problem  102, 115, 123, 158
empty object  23
Fibonacci numbers  13, 16, 141, 148, 154, 160, 162, 164
Fibonacci recurrence  13, 15, 177
file update  78, 179
fixed value mode  21
Fortran  92, 142
four-queens problem  102, 117, 174
function  11, 23, 50
    constant  13
    dynamic  11
    mutable  11
    non-mutable  11
    static  11
    vs. procedure  23, 24
generate-and-test  101, 104
generator  13, 50, 150, 165
    dynamic  12
    fibonacci  16, 154
    functional usage  28
    heapsort  20, 22
    in mathematics  132
    inorder  47, 49
    instance of  17, 50, 141
    of matrix elements  95, 98
    of runs  70
    preorder  25, 27, 113

    procedural usage   28
    simulation of   139, 141
    static   12
    tag values   26, 68, 79, 82, 97
    towers of Hanoi   44
global variable   14
graph search   126
    informed   127
    node expansion   126
    uninformed   127
greedy evaluation   166
Hamming sequence   173, 179
heap property   17
heapsort   19, 177
heuristic information   128
Icon   15, 142, 180
    binary comparison   143
    co-expression   155
    compound expression   145
    conditional expression   142
    expression as generator   150
    generators and backtracking   156
    initial block   149
    iteration   144
    null value   143, 147
    procedure   146, 148
    reversible assignment   158
    selection   144
    static memory   149
    success/failure   142
    user-defined generator   153
information-control system   9
inorder traversal   45
Knuth transformation   29, 54, 113, 177
lazy evaluation   166, 180
local variable   16
Lucid   160, 180
machine learning   12, 180
matrix   92

density  95
    sparse  95
matrix multiplication  10, 93
    sparse  95
menages problem  175
merge
    of sorted lists  83
    three-way  74
    two-way  66
Modula-2  15, 177
n-queens problem  102, 109, 115, 122
null value  22
own variable  15
parse tree  29
Pascal
    value mode in  21
    variable mode in  21
Prolog  35
permutation  115, 179
    partial  115, 179
    rosary  175
plateau  32, 172
postorder traversal  45, 52
predicative specification  59
preorder traversal  25, 36, 37, 38, 53, 109, 112, 113, 140
prime numbers  171
proof  32
queens problem  101, 115, 122, 179
    minimal coverage  174
    safe minimal coverage  173
quicksort  177
requirements statement  32, 34
rosary permutation  175
run  66
set union  83
shortest path problem  112
side effect  14, 24
smoothsort  171, 177
Snobol4  142

software reuse  83
sorting  66
    by heapsort  19, 20, 22
    by merging  67
    by smoothsort  171
sparse matrix multiplication  95
specification
    by program itself  63
    formal  32, 33, 87
    of inorder traversal  45
    of postorder traversal  45
    of preorder traversal  37
    of sorting  33
    predicative  59, 67, 103
    purpose of  62
    recursive  37, 63
spelling checker  86
state transition  69, 179
stepwise refinement  178
suspend statement  16, 51
tag value  26, 68, 79, 82, 97, 178
telegram problem  172, 178
testing  33, 34
text formatter problem  57, 178
towers of Hanoi  11, 41
transformations  36, 178
    correctness-preserving  35
    justification of  35, 36
    library of  35, 36
    of procedure to generator  43, 46
traveling salesperson problem  118, 122, 126
two-way merge  66
Unix  165
    pipe  165, 180
    pipeline  165, 169
validation  32, 34
value mode  21
variable
    global  14

    local  16
    own  15
    persistent  51
    temporary  51
variable mode  21
verification  32, 33
    by logical proof  32, 63
    by mathematical proof  33, 34, 39, 65, 75, 77, 82
    by testing  33

## ELLIS HORWOOD SERIES IN COMPUTERS AND THEIR APPLICATIONS
*Series Editor:* IAN CHIVERS, Senior Analyst, The Computer Centre, King's College, London, and formerly Senior Programmer and Analyst, Imperial College of Science and Technology, University of London

| | |
|---|---|
| Rubin, T. | USER INTERFACE DESIGN FOR COMPUTER SYSTEMS |
| Rudd, A.S. | PRACTICAL USAGE OF ISPF DIALOG MANAGER |
| de Saram, H. | PROGRAMMING IN MICRO-PROLOG |
| Savic, D. & Goodsell, D. | APPLICATIONS PROGRAMMING WITH SMALLTALK/V |
| Schirmer, C. | PROGRAMMING IN C FOR UNIX |
| Schofield, C.F. | OPTIMIZING FORTRAN PROGRAMS |
| Sharp, J.A. | DATA FLOW COMPUTING |
| Sherif, M.A. | DATABASE PROJECTS |
| Smith & Sage | EDUCATION AND THE INFORMATION SOCIETY |
| Smith, J.M & Stutely, R. | SGML |
| Späth, H. | CLUSTER ANALYSIS ALGORITHMS |
| Späth, H. | CLUSTER DISSECTION AND ANALYSIS |
| Stratford-Collins, P. | ADA |
| Tizzard, K. | C FOR PROFESSIONAL PROGRAMMERS |
| Turner, S.J. | AN INTRODUCTION TO COMPILER DESIGN |
| Wexler, J. | CONCURRENT PROGRAMMING IN OCCAM 2 |
| Whiddett, R.J. | CONCURRENT PROGRAMMING FOR SOFTWARE ENGINEERS |
| Whiddett, R.J., Berry, R.E., Blair, G.S., Hurley, P.N., Nicol, P.J. & Muir, S.J. | UNIX |
| Xu, Duan-zheng | COMPUTER ANALYSIS OF SEQUENTIAL MEDICAL TRIALS |
| Yannakoudakis, E.J. & Hutton, P.J. | SPEECH SYNTHESIS AND RECOGNITION SYSTEMS |
| Zech, R. | FORTH |

## Computer Communications and Networking

| | |
|---|---|
| Currie, W.S. | LANS EXPLAINED |
| Deasington, R.J. | A PRACTICAL GUIDE TO COMPUTER COMMUNICATIONS AND NETWORKING, 2nd Edition |
| Deasington, R.J. | X.25 EXPLAINED, 2nd Edition |
| Henshall, J. & Shaw, S. | OSI EXPLAINED |
| Kauffels, F.-J. | PRACTICAL LANS ANALYSED |
| Kauffels, F.-J. | PRACTICAL NETWORKS ANALYSED |
| Kauffels, F.-J. | UNDERSTANDING DATA COMMUNICATIONS |
| Muftic, S. | SECURITY MECHANISMS FOR COMPUTER NETWORKS |

**DATE DUE**